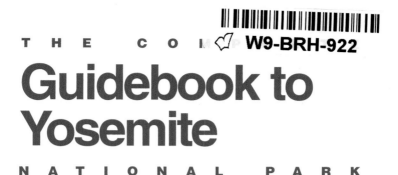
# THE COMPLETE
# Guidebook to Yosemite
## NATIONAL PARK

by Steven P. Medley

**Sixth Edition 2008**

**YOSEMITE ASSOCIATION**

Yosemite
National Park,
California

**HEYDAY BOOKS**

Heyday Books,
Berkeley,
California

*"On the whole, Yosemite is incomparably
the most wonderful feature on our continent."*
– A. D. Richardson

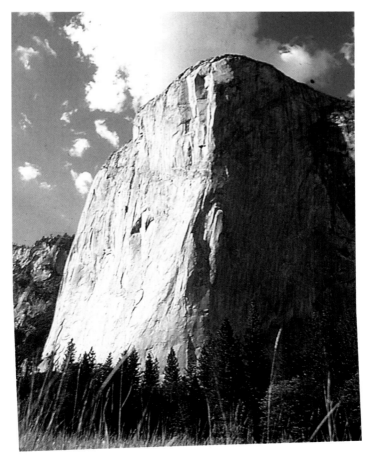

For Jane and the boys

*"From the discovery of Yosemite to the present day the wonders of this region of sublimity have been a source of inspiration to visitors, but none have been able to describe it to the satisfaction of those who followed after them."*—Lafayette Bunnell

*"You've got a good point Lafayette, but here goes anyway. . ."* —SPM

Orders, inquiries, and correspondence should be addressed to:
Heyday Books
P.O. Box 9145, Berkeley, CA 94709
(510) 549-3564, Fax (510) 549-1889
*www.heydaybooks.com*

Original book design by Jon Goodchild.

Revised book design and maps by Reineck & Reineck, San Francisco.

Illustrations by Bob Johnson.

Interior photographs courtesy of the National Park Service in Yosemite.

Front cover photograph by Jeff Grandy.

Printed in Singapore.

## Help Make This a Better Guidebook!

We are eager to hear your reactions to this book, and welcome your suggestions for additions or changes. Please send your commits, criticisms, and ideas to the Yosemite Association at the address above, or e-mail to: info@yosemite.org

## Further Reading

To purchase any of the books mentioned in this guidebook, visit the Yosemite Store Online at www.yosemitestore.com, or call (209) 379-2648.

## Acknowledgments

Thanks to everyone who helped in the production of this book, including Pat Wight, Penny Otwell, Holly Warner, Anne Steed, Laurel Rematore, Beth Pratt, Mary Vocelka, Ann Gushue, Jim Snyder, Linda Eade, Len McKenzie, Dean Shenk, Marla LaCass, Laurel Boyers, Craig Bates, N. King Huber, Jan van Wagtendonk, Peter Browning, Jim Alinder, Bill Neill, Mike Osborne, Mono Lake Committee, Keith Walklet, Nancy Lusignan, Kris Fister, Bob Jones, Tori Keith, Yosemite Concession Services, Jack and Gay Reineck, and Norma Craig.

## Caveat

Given the rapidity with which things change, the accuracy and completeness of the contents of this book cannot be guaranteed. The publisher and author assume no legal responsibility for the appreciation or depreciation of the value of any premises, commercial or otherwise, by reason of their inclusion in, or exclusion from this book. Further, the names of businesses mentioned here are provided as a service to readers and not as an endorsement or guarantee.

## Guidebook Update

This guidebook is regularly updated on the Internet at:
www.yosemite.org/member/update.htm.

# CONTENTS

# Major Features of Yosemite Valley

To Bridgeport

Toiyabe National Forest

Matterhorn Peak

Soldier Lake

Smedberg Lake

Spiller Lake

McCabe Lakes

Roosevelt Lake

Mt Conness

Young Lakes

Hwy 120 closed late fall- late spring west of this point

Hwy 395

Mono Lake

Hwy 120

Lee Vining

Glen Aulin High Sierra Camp

**Tuolumne Meadows**

Tioga Pass Entrance

Tuolumne Meadows Visitor Center

Dog Lake

Mt Dana
13053ft
3979m

Tioga Road

Lembert Dome

Tuolumne Lodge

Mt May Lake Sierra Camp

May Lake

Cathedral Peak

Elizabeth Lake

Lyell Fork

Mammoth Peak

Tenaya Lake

Evelyn Lake

Olmsted Point

Vogelsang High Sierra Camp

Clouds Rest

Sunrise High Sierra Camp

Bernice Lake

Merced River

Mt Lyell
13114ft
9997m

Inyo National Forest

Nevada Fall

Merced Lake

Washburn Lake

Merced Lake High Sierra Camp

Mt Clark

To Bishop

Ottoway Lakes

Edna Lake

Chain Lakes

Sierra National Forest

Roads

Trails

P Parking

R Restroom

Vista Point

Food

N

0        5 miles

## Yosemite by the Numbers

### Yosemite National Park
Established October 1, 1890

*Size:* 748,542 acres, or 1,169 square miles; 94% of the park is designated wilderness.

*Address:* P.O. Box 577, Yosemite National Park, CA 95389

*Campsites:* 1,445 individual sites parkwide

*Overnight Accommodations:* 1,729 units

*Paved Roads:* 360 miles

*Developed Trails:* 800 miles

*Wildlife Species* (approximate):
   Amphibians & Reptiles - 40
   Birds - 242
   Fish - 11
   Mammals - 77

*Flora Species:*
   Flowering Plants- 1,400
   Trees - 37

*Highest Peak:* Mt Lyell, 13,114 ft.

*Geographic Center of the Park:*
Mt Hoffmann

*Highest Paved Pass in the Sierra:*
Tioga Pass, 9,945 ft.

*Major Park Lakes:* 318
   With Fish - 127
   Without Fish – 191

*Rivers & Streams:* 880 miles

*Park Speed Limit:* 45 mph (unless otherwise posted)

### Yosemite's Ten Highest Peaks
1. Mt Lyell - 13,114 ft.
2. Mt Dana - 13,053 ft.
3. Kuna Peak - 13,003 ft.
4. Rodgers Peak - 12,978 ft.
5. Mt Maclure - 12,960 ft.
6. Mt Gibbs - 12,764 ft.
7. Mt Conness - 12,590 ft.
8. Mt Florence - 12,561 ft.
9. Simmons Peak - 12,503 ft.
10. Excelsior Mountain - 12,446 ft.

### Park Visitation
1855 - 42
1899 - 4,500
1922 - 100,506
1940 - 506,781
1954 - 1,008,031
1995 - 4,101,928
2000 - 3,550,065

### Entrance Fees
Private Noncommercial Vehicles: ......$20

Bus Passengers, Bicyclists, and Persons on Foot or Horseback: ........$10

Annual Yosemite Pass: ..................$40

National Parks Pass *(good at all national parks for one year from purchase date):* ...................$50

Golden Eagle Hologram for National Parks Pass *(covers entrance fees at other federal sites:* ........................$15

Golden Age Pass *(a lifetime pass for US citizens 62 years and older):* one-time issuance fee .....$10

Golden Access Pass *(for blind or permanently disabled U.S. citizens or permanent residents):* ......Free

### TDD Phones
These allow the hearing impaired with their own TDDs to call the park directly.

National Park
Service Information .........(209) 372-4726
Room Reservations .........(559) 255-8345
Camping Reservations .....(888) 530-9796

### Important Yosemite Phone Numbers
Unless otherwise noted, all phone numbers in this book are for the (209) area code.

Camping Reservations ....1-800-436-7275
(International Callers) .......(301) 772-1257

Dental Clinic ........................ 372-4200

High Sierra Camp
Reservations .................(559) 253-5674

Lost and Found .....................379-1002

Medical Clinic ......................372-4637

National Park Service .............372-0265

Park Information (recorded) .....372-0200

Room Reservations ........(559) 252-4848

Visitor Center, Big Oak Flat ......379-1899

Visitor Center,
Tuolumne Meadows .............372-0263

Visitor Center,
Yosemite Valley ...................372-0299

Wawona Ranger Station .........375-1416
                                 or 375-9520

Weather & Road Information ....372-0200

Wilderness Reservations .........372-0740

Yosemite Bookstore ...............379-2648

## If You Have Only One Day in Yosemite

*Three things only are well done in haste: flying from the plague, escaping quarrels, and catching flies.* — H. G. Bohn

If by some horrible twist of your itinerary you find yourself with but a single day in Yosemite National Park, you will be sorely cheated. The park is so large and so studded with fascinating features that usually three or four days are required to really "do the place justice." But take heart for there are some remarkable highlights that can be enjoyed in a day, many of them centered in Yosemite Valley.

### Yosemite Valley

While Yosemite Valley's seven square miles comprise but a tiny fraction of the park's total area, they are jam-packed with spectacular scenic beauty. First of all, get out of your car (follow signs to day-use parking at Camp 6 near Yosemite Village) and board a free Yosemite Valley Shuttle Bus. Buses stop at practically every point of interest in the eastern end of Yosemite Valley, and they are the only means (besides bicycle or on foot) to enter the areas there that are closed to automobile traffic. Listed below are several activities that can be enjoyed in a day from stops along the Shuttle Bus route. See page 27 for more Free Shuttle Bus information.

**Valley Visitor Center:** Here is a logical starting point for your visit. See page 26. Park information, an orientation film, exhibits, and books are all available here. If time allows, take in the Yosemite Museum Gallery, the Indian Cultural Exhibit, and walk through the Indian Village behind the center. (15 minutes to 1 hour)

**Lower Yosemite Fall:** Walk from the bus stop to the base of Lower Yosemite Fall— about a quarter of a mile. See page 32. Be prepared to get wet in spring when runoff is at its peak; in any season you'll be impressed by the imposing height of one of the world's most famous falls. (30 minutes to 1 hour)

**Happy Isles:** This is the trailhead for hikes to Vernal and Nevada Falls, Half Dome, and other high country destinations (except in winter). See page 32. Walk to the Vernal Fall bridge (seven-tenths of a mile) for a breathtaking view of this beautiful cataract, or continue on to the top of the fall (if you've got the energy). This route is known as the Mist Trail for reasons that will be obvious. During the summer, the Nature Center at Happy Isles offers exhibits and books. (1 to 3 hours)

**Mirror Lake:** From the shuttle bus stop (not accessible in winter), Mirror Lake is a half-mile walk up a slight grade. See page 32. While the lake no longer offers the mirror-like surface for which it was named (it's filling up with silt), one of the best views of Half Dome is had from its banks. The hike around the lake is easy and rewarding. (1 to 2 hours)

When you've seen and done all you want by shuttle bus, you will need your car to finish up in Yosemite Valley. For a thoroughly entertaining treatment of the remaining sights, an audio CD program entitled *Yosemite Audio Guides: Yosemite Valley Tour* is available for sale at the Visitor Center and heartily recommended. The tour consists of ten stops and, besides descriptions of the scenery, features discussions of geology, Native American culture, history, and park management. The CD is exceptionally well-produced. Using it, you will require from 2 to 4 hours for your tour depending on how much exploring you do at each stop.

If you don't use the CD, there are at least two more Yosemite Valley points to visit:

**Bridalveil Fall:** Follow road signs to the Wawona Road (to Wawona and Fresno). Immediately after turning on to the Wawona Road, turn left into the Bridalveil Fall parking lot. The short trail leads to the base of the fall where a sheet of water floats downward 620 feet to the valley floor. (15 to 45 minutes)

*Bridalveil Fall*

**Tunnel View:** Turn left back onto the Wawona Road and drive approximately three miles to Tunnel View turnout, which is just below the entrance to the Wawona Tunnel. Before you is the classic panoramic view of Yosemite Valley that greeted the first visitors here. (10 to 30 minutes)

**Glacier Point**

A 32-mile drive from Yosemite Valley, Glacier Point is unquestionably a "must see" for visitors with limited time. Within 200 yards of the parking lot is the top of the sheer southern wall of Yosemite Valley. Not only does the valley lie 3,200 feet below you, but also the entire park is revealed with astounding vistas in every direction. Most of Yosemite's major peaks are identified, and exhibits explain the geologic processes that created this amazing landscape. There is probably no better view of Yosemite Valley and the surrounding high country that can be reached by automobile. The road to Glacier Point is closed in winter. See page 46 for more information. (1 hour for the drive from Yosemite Valley, and 30 minutes to 1 hour at Glacier Point)

**Mariposa Grove of Big Trees**

If you have already seen Yosemite Valley and Glacier Point and you've still got time (hard to believe!), the Mariposa Grove of Big Trees is located near the park's south entrance from Highway 41. See page 48. This magnificent stand of sequoias is Yosemite's largest and includes trees thousands of years old. A tram system transports visitors into the grove for a fee (from May to October), or you may enter on foot (the hike into the upper grove area is fairly rigorous, however). A small museum is open during the summer (the tram stops there), and famous trees like the Grizzly Giant and the fallen Tunnel Tree should not be missed. (2 to 3 hours)

**Tuolumne Meadows and the Tioga Road**

Open in summer only, the Tioga Road bisects the park and leads through Tuolumne Meadows, a beautiful subalpine meadow surrounded by soaring granite crags and polished domes. See page 65. If your trip takes you out of the park to the east, the Tioga Road is lined with scenery and exhibits describing it. See page 60. Be sure to stop at Olmsted Point for its remarkable view of Tenaya Canyon and the back side of Half Dome, and of Tenaya Lake, the deep-blue, icy-cold waters of which form Yosemite's largest natural lake. (Allow 2 to 2$^1$/$_2$ hours for the trip from Yosemite Valley to Tioga Pass)

**Just Passing Through?**

If it happens that you are simply driving through Yosemite (a regrettable situation), be sure to pick up a copy of the *Yosemite Road Guide* that will provide an added dimension to your drive. It is keyed to markers along park roads and describes the sights, gives historical information, and is full of data about Yosemite's plants and animals.

## Lodging in Yosemite

*M*ost overnight accommodations in Yosemite are operated by Delaware North Company Parks & Resorts at Yosemite (DNC), a contractor of the National Park Service and the park's chief concessioner. There is a single reservation system for all DNC lodging units. Whenever a Yosemite hotel or motel is not part of the DNC reservation system, that fact will be noted in this guidebook.

Reservations may be made by phone, over the Internet, or through the mail. The DNC reservation number is (559) 252-4848. Because thousands of calls are made to this number each day, you may not get through when you phone. Be persistent, let the phone ring, and try, try again.

Better yet, use the Internet. A percentage of the concessioner's lodging units are available only through its web site. If you've got a credit card, visit www.yosemitepark.com to request your reservation online.

If you're still not successful, try sending your reservation request in writing. Fill out the form provided below and mail it to: Yosemite Reservations, 5410 E. Home, Fresno, CA 93722. Be sure to indicate acceptable alternatives, as competition for popular dates is heavy.

### Nine Tips for Getting a Yosemite Reservation

1 Public reservations for Yosemite lodging open exactly 366 days in advance. Call (559) 252-4848 immediately upon the opening of the Yosemite Reservations office (8 a.m. Pacific time) exactly 366 days before your intended arrival.

2 Choose to visit in Yosemite's off season, particularly the months of November, January, February, and March. You're sure to be accommodated if you elect to come during the week. There's a special winter reservation number: (559) 454-2000.

3 If you want to stay over a weekend, plan your arrival for a Monday, Tuesday, Wednesday, or Thursday. You can reserve up to seven nights in a row in any given stay. Often, lodging facilities are fully reserved for weekends more than 366 days in advance by people arriving earlier in the week.

4 Be flexible and have several arrival dates in mind. If your first option is not available, one of the others may be.

5 If you're willing to stay in a tent cabin at Curry Village, request it. Tent cabins are in the least demand and can usually be reserved up to two weeks before arrival. And when you arrive, you can always try to upgrade to a room with bath (but there are no guarantees here).

6 Call Yosemite Reservations on Saturday or Sunday. The office receives the fewest numbers of calls on weekends. Don't call at lunch. Everybody tries to call then.

7 Take advantage of the fact that some lodging units can only be reserved online. Visit www.yosemitepark.com if you're not having success over the phone.

8 Call 30 days, 15 days, or 7 days in advance of your arrival. These are common times when rooms held by previous reservations are cancelled. You may get lucky.

9 If you arrive in Yosemite without a reservation, stop by the front desk of any lodging facility between 10 a.m. and 4 p.m. and place your name on the waiting list. Persons with reservations that are held without a deposit must confirm or arrive by 4 p.m. If they don't, their reservations are cancelled automatically. If you are present at 4 p.m. you may pick up a cancelled reservation or you may not.

### Reservations for Lodging

*Reservations Request Form (please print)*

Name

Address

| City | State | Zip |
| --- | --- | --- |

| Number in Party | Children | Ages |
| --- | --- | --- |

Preferred accommodation

| Date of Arrival | Date of Departure |
| --- | --- |

Number of Nights

2nd Choice, if preference is unavailable

Mail to: **Yosemite Reservations** 5410 East Home, Fresno, CA 93727

## Camping in Yosemite National Park

Yosemite National Park offers visitors almost 1,500 campsites in its multiple campgrounds. If you're planning to camp, be sure to secure an authorized spot because camping is allowed only in designated campsites. Even if you've got a "self-contained" recreational vehicle, you are not permitted to pull off to the side of the road for the night. Neither should you erect your tent or throw down a sleeping bag wherever you stop; the rangers will send you packing. The impact on the park resources of such haphazard camping is too great.

Fortunately, there's a way to ensure that you'll have a Yosemite camping spot when you arrive. The majority of park campsites can be reserved through a campground reservation system administered by National Park Reservation System (NPRS). Throughout this guidebook, campgrounds with sites that can be reserved through NPRS are indicated.

### How to Reserve Your Campsite

Campground reservations are available in one-month blocks up to five months in advance. They can be made on the 15th of each month for this one month "window" through NPRS. For example, on March 15, dates from August 15 through September 14 become available for reservation, and on April 15, dates from September 15 through October 14 are reservable.

You may reserve campsites through NPRS in three ways: by mail, over the Internet, and using the telephone. For telephone reservations, you should call (800) 436-7275. The number for international callers is (301) 722-1257. Phone reservations may be made between 7 a.m. and 7 p.m. Pacific time.

The system allows callers to choose from a full month of starting dates for their camping trip. This should do away with the previous arrangement where multiple phone calls had to be made if certain dates weren't available. Be sure to pick a number of possible start dates for your trip and you should be able to secure a reservation.

Online camping reservations can be made at reservations.nps.gov, but you may reserve only one campsite at a time using this system. This Internet service is only available between 7 a.m. and 7 p.m. Pacific time. Another web site, www.yosemitesites.com, provides helpful information about how many sites are available in each campground and still reservable.

To reserve by mail, fill out a copy of the form provided here and send it to: NPRS, P.O. Box 1600, Cumberland, MD 21502. You should time the mailing of your request so that it is received no sooner than two weeks before the 15th of the month that your desired camping arrival date goes on sale. Written requests will not be processed until the 15th of the month (at the same time that telephone requests are taken).

For additional information about park campgrounds, refer to the following pages:

Yosemite Valley, page 34
South of Yosemite Valley, page 51
North of Yosemite Valley, page 68

### Camping in US Forest Service Areas Adjacent to Yosemite

The US Forest Service operates a variety of campgrounds near Yosemite. Many of them are operated on a first-come, first-served basis; some sites may be reserved in advance. For additional information, call the appropriate USFS district office.

**Inyo National Forest**
Eastern Sierra, Highways 120 & 395
Mono Lake Ranger Station
(760) 647-3044

**Sierra National Forest**
Western Sierra, Highways 140 & 41
Bass Lake Ranger District
Oakhurst Ranger Station
(559) 683-4636

Mariposa Ranger Station
(209) 966-3638

**Stanislaus National Forest**
Western Sierra, Highway 120
Groveland Ranger Station
(209) 962-7825

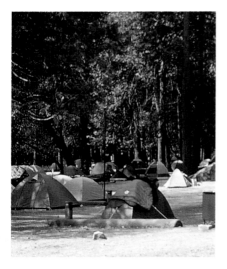

## Camping in Yosemite National Park

**Valleywide stay limit:** 7 days
**High country stay limit:** 14 days
30 day stay limit per calendar year

| Campground/general location | number of sites or spaces | daily fee: per site=/s per person=/p | RV space | tent space | tap water | stream water (boil) | flush toilets | pit toilets | tables | fire pits or grills | pets allowed | dump station | parking | showers nearby | laundry nearby | groceries | swimming | fishing | horseback riding | camping season (approximate) | |
|---|---|---|---|---|---|---|---|---|---|---|---|---|---|---|---|---|---|---|---|---|---|
| North Pines Yosemite Valley | 84 | $18/s | ● | ● | ● | | ● | | ● | ● | ● | ● | ● | ● | ● | ● | ● | ● | ● | Apr-Sept | NPRS |
| Upper Pines Yosemite Valley | 238 | $18/s | ● | ● | ● | | ● | | ● | ● | ● | ● | ● | ● | ● | ● | ● | ● | ● | all year | NPRS |
| Lower Pines Yosemite Valley | 60 | $18/s | ● | ● | ● | | ● | | ● | ● | ● | ● | ● | ● | ● | ● | ● | ● | ● | Mar-Oct | NPRS |
| Sunnyside-Walk In Yosemite Valley | 35 | $5/p | | ● | ● | | ● | | ● | ● | | | ● | ● | ● | ● | ● | ● | ● | all year | First come basis. Limited parking. |
| Backpackers Walk-In Yosemite Valley | 25 | $5/p | | ● | | ● | | ● | ● | ● | | | | ● | ● | ● | ● | ● | ● | May-Oct | First come basis. No vehicles. Two night max. |
| Wawona Wawona Road in Wawona | 93 | $18/s | ● | ● | ● | | ● | | ● | ● | ● | ● | ● | | | | ● | ● | ● | | NPRS from May-Sept. ($18/s); first come basis from Oct-April ($12/s) |
| Bridalveil Creek Glacier Point Road | 110 | $12/s | ● | ● | | | | ● | ● | ● | | | ● | | | | | ● | ● | July-Sept | First come basis |
| Hogdon Meadow off Big Oak Flat Road near entrance | 105 | $18/s | ● | ● | ● | | ● | | ● | ● | ● | ● | ● | | | | | | ● | all year | NPRS from May-Sept ($18/s); first come basis from Oct-April ($12/s) |
| Hetch Hetchy Backpacker Hetch Hetchy Road | 19 | $5/p $50/s | | ● | ● | | | ● | ● | ● | | | ● | | | | ● | ● | ● | | Apr-Nov | First come basis. Two group sites, two stock use sites. Wilderness users only. No RV. |
| Crane Flat Big Oak Flat Road nr Tioga Road turnoff | 166 | $18/s | ● | ● | ● | | ● | | ● | ● | ● | ● | ● | | | ● | | | | June-Sept | NPRS |
| Tamarack Flat Tioga Road | 52 | $8/s | ● | ● | | ● | | ● | ● | ● | | | ● | | | | | | | June-Sept | First come basis. No RV. |
| White Wolf Tioga Road | 74 | $12/s | ● | ● | ● | | ● | | ● | ● | | | ● | | | | | ● | | July-Sept | First come basis. No RVs over 27 feet. |
| Yosemite Creek Tioga Road | 75 | $8/s | ● | ● | | ● | | ● | ● | ● | | | ● | | | | | ● | | July-Sept | First come basis. No RV. |
| Porcupine Flat Tioga Road | 52 | $8/s | ● | ● | | ● | | ● | ● | ● | | | ● | | | | | | | July-Sept | First come basis. Limited RV |
| Tuolumne Meadows Tioga Road | 304 | $18/s | ● | ● | ● | | ● | | ● | ● | ● | ● | ● | | | ● | | ● | ● | July-Sept | NPRS advanced reservations for half of campground; same-day reservations for rest. 25 walk-in sites with no vehicles, $5/p. |

**NPRS:** reservations required. **NO RV:** access road not suitable for trailers or large RVs.

# Campsite Reservation Request

Please include middle initial in your name:

Name:

Address:

Zip: _____ Telephone: _____

No. of Persons: _____ Pets(s): ☐ Yes ☐ No

**National Park Reservation Service**
P.O. Box 1600, Cumberland, MD 21501

If necessary, will you accept fewer nights? ☐ Yes ☐ No

Specific campsites cannot be reserved.
Campsites are assigned upon arrival.

Be sure you complete all sections and enclose full payment.
Incomplete or incorrect forms will be returned.

**Type of camping equipment:**

| Check ✓ | | |
|---|---|---|
| 1 | One tent or no equipment | |
| 2 | Two tents | |
| 3 | Large tent (over 9' x 12') | |
| 4 | Tent trailer, total length?: | |
| 5 | Van or bus with side tent | |
| 6 | Pickup/camper thru 21' | |
| 7 | Pickup/camper thru 24' | |
| 8 | Motorhome thru 24' | |
| 9 | Motorhome thru 27' | |
| 10 | Motorhome over 27' ( ft) | |
| 11 | Trailer thru 15' | |
| 12 | Trailer thru 18' | |
| 13 | Trailer thru 21' | |
| 14 | Trailer thru 24' | |
| 15 | Trailer thru 27' | |
| 16 | Trailer over 27' ( ft) | |
| ♿ | | 17 |
| | | 18 |
| | | 19 |
| | | 20 |
| | | 21 |
| | | 22 |
| | | 23 |
| | | 24 |
| | | 25 |
| | | 26 |
| | | 27 |
| | | 28 |
| | | 29 |
| | | 30 |
| | | 31 |
| | | 32 |

Golden Access or Golden Age Passport
Serial No. if applicable

*Not Golden eagle Passport or Park Pass*

**Charges:** The daily campsite charge is required for each period and/or campsite, up to the stay limit.

No. of nights _____ @ _____ * = _____

No. of nights _____ @ _____ * = _____

No. of nights _____ @ _____ * = _____ **Total:**

*50% reduction for Golden Access
or Golden Age Passport

☐ Check/MO ☐ Discover ☐ MasterCard ☐ Visa

Card No.: _____ Exp: _____

Cardholder: _____ Telephone _____

Signature: _____

Make payable to NPS and mail to:
NPRS, P.O. Box 1600, Cumberland, MD 21501

| Name of Park | Campground | First Choice Arrival Dates | Nights | Second Choice Arrival Dates | Nights | Third Choice Arrival Dates | Nights | Official Use |
|---|---|---|---|---|---|---|---|---|
| | | | | | | | | |
| | | | | | | | | |
| | | | | | | | | |

## So How's the Weather?

*"There is really no such thing as bad weather, only different kinds of good weather."* —John Ruskin

Yosemite's climate is as mild as its cliffs are steep. The months of April through October feature warm daytime temperatures and cool nights. Even winter is relatively benign with average maximum temperatures in Yosemite Valley (4,000 feet) in the high 40s and 50s. Of course weather is significantly affected by elevation, and with a topography ranging from 2,000 to 13,000 feet in height, Yosemite can experience amazing climatic variations on any given day!

Precipitation averages 35 to 40 inches of moisture annually, with the greatest bulk of that falling between December and March. Snowfall in Yosemite Valley averages 29 inches, but rarely accumulates to a depth of over two feet. At 7,000 foot Badger Pass, there is adequate snow pack to support a downhill ski area, and cross-country skiing is popular throughout the higher regions of the park. As temperatures warm in the spring, increasing runoff swells rivers and creeks producing a grand display of surging waterfalls. There is negligible precipitation during the summer months, and many of the park's waterfalls literally dry up.

### Yosemite Valley in Winter

The first falls of snow in the Sierra generally occur in November, but they do not come to stay; they are but fleeting messengers, and having announced the approach of winter, are soon put to flight by the lingering god of the tropics, who still tries to maintain supremacy over his rival of the Arctic Zone. But it is his final effort to keep back the legions of the north. By the end of December snow hides from sight all but the forms of the mountains, covering them with a vast winding sheet. Only the mighty trees toss from their wind-shaken branches the white deposit, which ofttimes with its unyielding weight snaps their great boughs.

Owing to the retreat of the sun southward, and the immense height of the walls of the Yosemite, there is a considerable difference between the climate on the north and south side of the valley during the winter. While on the south wall the sun never shines during this season, and a chilling shadow is constantly cast over that portion of the valley, the rays of the winter sun fall upon the surface of the northern elevation almost at right angles with its plane. As a consequence, the weather on that side is mellow and mild, and in sheltered nooks among the warm rocks flowers are observed to bloom every month in the year.

From *Foley's Yosemite Souvenir & Guide* for 1913 by D. J. Foley.

## Yosemite Valley Weather Data

| | Jan | Feb | Mar | Apr | May | June | July | Aug | Sept | Oct | Nov | Dec |
|---|---|---|---|---|---|---|---|---|---|---|---|---|
| **Rainfall\*** *in inches* | 6.2 | 6.1 | 5.2 | 3.0 | 1.3 | 0.7 | 0.4 | 0.3 | 0.9 | 2.1 | 5.5 | 5.6 |
| **Max. Temp.** | 49 | 55 | 59 | 65 | 73 | 82 | 90 | 90 | 87 | 74 | 58 | 48°F |
| **Min. Temp.** | 26 | 28 | 31 | 35 | 42 | 48 | 54 | 53 | 47 | 39 | 31 | 26°F |

*\*37.2 inches annually*

| | January | April | July | October |
|---|---|---|---|---|
| **Hours of Sunshine** | 3:57 | 7:38 | 9:34 | 6:45 |
| **Chances of a Sunny Day** | 39% | 70% | 97% | 81% |
| **Afternoon Temperatures** | 48° | 66° | 90° | 75° |
| **Relative Humidity** | 86% | 69% | 50% | 64% |
| **Chances of a Dry Day** | 74% | 80% | 97% | 94% |
| **Total Precipitation** | 6.8" | 3.3" | 0.4" | 1.5" |
| **Snowfall** | 25.4" | 4.5" | – | 0.2" |

**Comment:** High country conditions are significantly cooler and much snowier during the winter months.

### Online Weather Forecast

For the latest weather conditions for the Sierra Nevada from Yosemite to Kings Canyon, visit the following web site: http://www.wrh.noaa.gov/afos/SplitData/SFO/ZFP/ZFPCAZ096

## Backpacking in Yosemite

*B*ecause there are some 800 miles of trail in Yosemite ranging through some of the most stunning scenery in the world, backpacking is a popular activity in the park. It allows its practitioners a true wilderness experience, and is really the only way large areas of Yosemite can be reached.

But successful, minimum impact backpacking requires good physical health, knowledge of backpacking techniques, proper equipment, and a respect for the natural world. Uninformed backcountry users can cause great harm to the wilderness and not even know it. What follows are basic tips for back packers, wilderness regulations, and sources for further information.

### Get A Wilderness Permit

Free wilderness permits are required year-round for all overnight stays in Yosemite's backcountry. To avoid overcrowding and reduce impacts to wilderness areas, Yosemite limits the number of people who may begin overnight hikes from each trailhead each day. At least 40% of each trailhead quota is available on a first-come, first-served basis the day of, or one day prior to, the beginning of your trip.

These permits may be obtained at any of the following locations in the park: the Wilderness Center in Yosemite Valley (just east of the Visitor Center), Tuolumne Meadows Permit Kiosk (just off the Tioga Road on the road to Tuolumne Lodge), Wawona Information Center (see page 42), Big Oak Flat Visitor Center (see page 57), and Hetch Hetchy Entrance Station for those using Hetch Hetchy trails (see Page 57).

Wilderness permit reservations can now be made year-round, from up to twenty-four weeks to two days in advance. Those desiring a reservation can visit the Wilderness Center in Yosemite Valley, mail in a reservation request, visit the Wilderness Reservation web site at www.yosemitesecure.org/wildpermit/, or call the center at (209) 372-0740. A $5 per person, non-refundable fee is charged for reservations. Fees may be paid by check (payable to "Yosemite Association") or with a major credit card including expiration date.

The following information is needed to process a wilderness permit or reservation: name, address, daytime phone; number of people in group; method of travel (i.e., ski, snowshoe, foot, horse); starting and ending dates of hike; the entry and exit trailhead you use; your primary destination; number of pack stock (if applicable); alternative dates or trailheads if your first choice isn't available. Mail requests should be sent to Wilderness Center, PO Box 545, Yosemite, CA 95389.

Permits may be picked up no more than 24 hours prior to trailhead departure. Reservations are especially recommended for hikes leaving from Tuolumne Meadows or with destinations of Little Yosemite Valley, Half Dome, or Merced Lake, and for any hikers planning a Saturday night stay.

### Wilderness Regulations

**Group Size:** Maximum group size in the Yosemite Wilderness is 15 people on trails and 8 people maximum for any off-trail travel.

**Campsite Location:** Please use existing campsites at least 100 feet from lakeshores and streams to minimize pollution and vegetation impact. Camp four trail-miles from Tuolumne Meadows, Yosemite Valley, Glacier Point, White Wolf, Hetch Hetchy, and Wawona, and at least one trail-mile from any road.

**Human Waste:** Bury human waste six inches deep in a small hole at least 100 feet from any lake, stream, or camp area. Toilet paper should be burned or packed out.

**Garbage:** Pack out all garbage (no exceptions). Do not bury garbage, scatter organic waste, or leave foil in campfire sites.

**Fires:** Use gas stoves rather than wood fires. Wood fires are not permitted above 9,600 feet due to firewood scarcity. Use only existing fire rings and dead and down wood in areas below 9,600 feet.

**Pets:** Dogs and other pets are not allowed in the Yosemite wilderness.

**Soap:** Putting soap, including bio-degradable soap, or any form of pollutant into lakes or streams is prohibited. Discard wash and rinse water at least 100 feet from water sources.

**Firearms:** Firearms are not permitted in the wilderness.

### Route Planning Information

Space considerations prevent a listing of even some of the thousands of trips that can be made into the Yosemite wilderness. But never fear, there are many resources available to help with your route planning task. You can obtain maps or any of the trail guides listed on page 17 from the Yosemite Association, at the Wilderness Center, at one of the Visitor Center bookstores, through the Yosemite Bookstore online at www.yosemitestore.com, or through the mail by writing PO Box 230, El Portal, CA 95318, or calling (209) 379-2648.

## Wilderness Tips

**Visit the Wilderness Center:** At the Wilderness Center, just east of the Visitor Center on the pedestrian mall in Yosemite Valley, detailed information is available about the park's wilderness, there are educational displays, a trip planning sect-ion is provided, and guidebooks, maps, and backpacker supplies are offered for sale. For additional information, visit the NPS wilderness information web site at www.nps.gov/yose/wilderness.

**Key Phone Numbers:**
Wilderness permit reservations (209) 372-0740

Current wilderness conditions (209) 372-0307

For more information about making reservation or obtaining a permit call (209) 372-0310.

**Treat the Water:** Unfortunately, microscopic organisms known as *Giardia lamblia* (see page 92) are present in wilderness lakes, rivers, and streams. They can cause illness (sometimes quite severe), so you should not drink from these sources without first treating the water. Your options are to boil it for three minutes, to use a chemical disinfectant like iodine or chlorine (less effective than boiling), or to use a Giardia-rated water filter available from outdoor equipment stores, at the Wilderness Center, or from the Yosemite Store online at www.yosemitestore.com.

**Get Acclimatized:** Many wilderness trips begin at elevations much higher than you may be accustomed to and then go even higher. It's a good idea to arrive a day early to let your body adapt to the thinner air. Don't over-exert, and drink plenty of fluids to avoid altitude sickness.

## Bear-Proof Your Campsite

Yosemite's black bears are clever and very persistent. If you fail to set up your camp and store your food properly, your whole trip can be ruined. Always follow these six steps:

**1. Use the food storage boxes** at your trailhead for keeping any food that you will not be taking on your backpack trip. Never leave food or food-related supplies in vehicles left overnight at trailheads.

**2. Store your food** in a bear-resistant food storage container. Weighing just 2.9 pounds and holding from 5 to 7 days worth of food for one person, the canisters are strongly encouraged by the National Park Service, and required above 9,600 feet. They are for sale and rent at the Wilderness Center, the Curry Village Mountain Shop, and the Village Sports Shop in Yosemite Valley, at the Crane Flat Store, at the Tuolumne Reservation Cabin and the Mountaineering School in Tuolumne Meadows, at the Wawona Information Station and the Wawona Store, at the Big Oak Flat Information Station, and at the Hetch Hetchy Information Station.

**3. Hang your food** and anything with an odor as instructed by the NPS if you don't use a canister. Hang pots and pans from food bags as an alarm. Sleep 20 to 30 feet from where you hang items so you can hear the bear and scare it away as quickly as possible.

**4. If a bear approaches** your camp, act immediately to scare it away. Yell and make as much noise as possible. Throw small rocks no larger than golf balls at the bear. Make noise and chase the bear. Multiple people chasing a bear increases effectiveness.

**5. Always maintain a distance.** Do not advance on a bear that appears to feel threatened or cornered by you. Do not attempt to retrieve food or gear from a bear until the item is abandoned.

**6. Food taken by bears** is your responsibility. Please clean up and report all bear damage to a ranger. Improper food storage can result in the killing of conditioned bears, personal injury, and property loss. Please do your part to keep Yosemite's bears wild.

## Further Reading

*Yosemite National Park: A Natural History Guide to Yosemite and Its Trails* by Jeffrey P. Schaffer. Berkeley: Wilderness Press, 1989.

*High Sierra Hiking Guides for Hetch Hetchy, Tuolumne Meadows, and Yosemite* by various authors. Berkeley: Wilderness Press, various dates.

*Guide to the John Muir Trail* by Thomas Winnett. Berkeley: Wilderness Press, 1984.

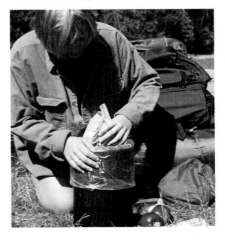

## Yosemite Climbing

Because of its granite landscape, Yosemite is mecca for rock climbers from all over the United States and the world. Yosemite Valley has been the location of so many climbing developments and innovations that it has become the yardstick against which all other climbing areas are measured. In every season of the year, climbers can be seen clinging to rock faces or hanging by their hands and feet from upward-leading cracks.

Passionate rock climbers populate a world foreign to most "normal" people, and have developed a subculture with customs, clothing, language, and tools of its own. In Yosemite, that world revolves around Camp Four (known on signs and maps as Sunnyside Campground). Across Northside Drive from Yosemite Lodge, Camp Four is the climbers' permanent temporary home. Many of the hard core climbers move to Tuolumne Meadows during the summer.

Not that long ago, climbers utilized many artificial techniques to accomplish their climbs. These included drilling holes in the rock and inserting permanent metal bolts, chiseling holds in the rocks, and hammering in steel "pitons" that damaged the rock and might not be removable. Such steps made certain routes climbable that might not otherwise be.

Today, a less destructive and harmful climbing ethic has developed. Bolts are placed much less often, chiseling is frowned upon, and high-tech devices like "chocks," "friends," and "cams" (that are inserted into cracks and removed easily) provide protection for modern climbers. It's known as clean climbing, and it's a matter of high priority for climbers who wish to protect and preserve a natural, non-artificial climbing environment.

One interesting aspect of the climbing subculture is its system of naming and rating climbing routes. The first climber to successfully undertake a new path up a section of rock (a "first ascent") is entitled to name that route. That climber, and those who come after, attempt to rate the difficulty of climbing that route. The Yosemite Decimal System is used for this purpose and is an elaborate scale with ratings from 5.0 to 5.13 with grades from "a" to "d" at each level signifying different degrees of difficulty to the climbing community.

Climbs range from short routes of 50 feet or less (a pitch) to multi-day ascents of Yosemite's biggest walls (like El Capitan), which are made up of many pitches. A number of practitioners of the sport are now engaged in what is known as "free soloing." Not recommended for other than the finest, most skilled climbers, free soloing is the climbing of rocks without the assistance and protection of a climbing partner. Generally, no ropes are used, no climbing devices are attached to the rock, and no one will be there to catch you if you fall. Most of Yosemite's largest rock landmarks have been "free soloed" in less than a day.

The technology of climbing has advanced considerably over the past several decades. Special ropes made from synthetic fibers are used, and they stretch to absorb the weight of a falling climber. Their strength under pressure has also increased. Shoes covered with sticky rubber that adheres to practically any surface are now commonly used. And the devices mentioned above like cams and friends made from high-strength alloys have expanded climbing opportunities as well.

But good equipment or not, climbers must still have the skill and strength to climb the rocks. The mastery that has been achieved by many "rock jocks" is astounding, and routes that many once considered unclimbable are now accomplished almost daily. New routes are being explored and climbed, and other climbing firsts, like paraplegic Mark Wellman's 1989 ascent of El Capitan, continue to occur.

Rock climbing is not recommended for the casual park visitor. If you would like to learn more about the sport, consider taking a lesson from the Yosemite Mountaineering School either in Yosemite Valley (call 372-8344) or in Tuolumne Meadows (summer only call 372-8435). Without proper equipment and without proper technique, you could severely injure yourself or die.

### Ten Very Curious Names for Yosemite Climbing Routes
Agricultural Maneuvers in the Dark (5.8)
Chairman Ted Scraps the Time Machine (5.10a)
Colony of Slippermen (5.11d)
Dope Smoking Moron (5.11)
Gerbil Launcher (5.10d)
God Told Me to Skin You Alive (5.11a)
Public Enema Number One (5.11c)
Stand and Quiver (5.11a)
Tooth or Consequences (5.11b)
Vegetal Extraction (5.10)

## A Ranger is a Ranger is a....

*Oh, the ranger's life is full of joys,*
*And they're all good, jolly, care-free boys,*
*And in wealth they are sure to roll and reek,*
*For a ranger can live on one meal a week.*
—Anonymous

Yosemite National Park is administered by the US National Park Service (NPS), an agency of the Department of the Interior established in 1916. As a bureaucracy based loosely on a military model, the NPS is characterized by a complex ordering of job ranks and by its distinctive field uniforms. The green pants, gray shirt, and universally recognized "Smokey the Bear" hat have become the trademark of the park ranger. The key descriptor here is "park" as park rangers differ from forest rangers. Forest rangers work for the US Forest Service, a branch of the US Department of Agriculture, in national forests throughout the country. While the job duties of park and forest rangers are often similar in their respective situations, park rangers work in parks and monuments, and forest rangers work in _____ (you fill in the blank!).

Now that you're able to recognize that the person in the flat-brimmed hat before you is a park ranger working in a national park, things start to get a bit more complicated. The National Park Service is divided into any number of departments ranging from visitor protection to interpretation to maintenance to resources management to administration. To confuse things, employees of the different divisions all wear roughly the same uniform. The traditional park ranger is employed by the Division of Visitor Protection, with duties that include law enforcement, traffic regulation, search and rescue, emergency medical treat-ment, and many others. In order to work as a traditional (or "real") park ranger, one must take special training and earn a law enforcement commission.

Park interpreters (interpretive rangers, formerly called naturalists) are responsible for the educational program at

PARK RANGER

Yosemite, and give walks, talks, and programs. They, too, are "real" rangers, but they generally have not been commissioned and do not perform law enforcement functions. Their uniforms are identical to those of protection rangers (except they don't carry guns and handcuffs).

Identical, too, are the outfits of the various park administrators like the Superintendent (the park's chief administrative officer), Deputy Superintendent, Chief Ranger, and other division chiefs. An easy way to distinguish these management types is by their skin pallor. They attend so many government meetings they almost never see the sun.

Things get a little more confusing with certain maintenance, fire, and resource management workers. They've got the green pants, ditto the gray shirt, but instead of the funny hat, they wear dark green baseball caps with the NPS arrowhead insignia. These employees are not technically rangers, but their roles at Yosemite are equally significant and their contributions considerable.

Most people don't realize that the National Park Service has "exclusive jurisdiction" over Yosemite National Park. That means that state, county, and local agencies do not operate and provide almost no traditional services here. In Yosemite there are no highway patrol officers, no sheriff's officers, no state or municipal firefighters, no state courts, and no incorporated local government. These services fall to the National Park Service, which very ably manages the park.

Please remember while you're in the park that if you need help of any kind (from emergency assistance to information), all uniformed NPS personnel are there to be of service.

**Q:** Who was Yosemite's first ranger?

**A:** Archie O. Leonard, hired in 1898, was the original "civilian" park ranger in the park. Government-hired rangers began in 1914, and the National Park Service was created in 1916.

## Yosemite in Winter

*M*any have the impression that when the first day of winter arrives in Yosemite, the whole place closes up tight until spring. They are mistaken, however; the park and its residents do not hibernate. Yosemite only "closes" when deep snowfall makes it impossible to plow access roads (which is almost never).

There are notable park changes in winter, but most of them add to the unique qualities of this special season. Much of Yosemite wears a covering of snow, and once-thundering waterfalls quiet themselves in frozen dormancy. The Tioga and Glacier Point Roads close, and visitor activities center on such winter sports as skiing and skating.

Weekdays in winter are perfect for experiencing Yosemite in a less crowded, more serene environment. Yosemite Valley daytime temperatures can be surprisingly mild, and winter walks are some of the best. The biggest reward of all, however, is the sheer beauty and grandeur of a transfigured Yosemite and its surrounding high country.

The major routes to the park remain open throughout the year. The roadway least affected by the weather is Highway 140 which leads from Merced via Mariposa and through the Arch Rock Entrance to the park. Highways 120 (from the west) and 41 are also excellent routes, but they are more often subject to closure from heavy snowfall, and many times require the use of tire chains. The roads in Yosemite Valley are plowed throughout the winter.

Winter driving in Yosemite requires special precautions. Because roads are regularly covered with ice and snow, driving speeds should be reduced. Always carry tire chains in your vehicle and obey the chain requirement signs. Watch out for snowplows, and never stop in the roadway (find a pullout where traffic can safely pass).

### Skiing and Snowboarding

Both cross-country types and downhillers will discover ski and snowboard opportunities in Yosemite. California's oldest operating ski area, Badger Pass, is located at 7,300 feet about 45 minutes from Yosemite Valley on the Glacier Point Road. It's primarily a "family" oriented operation with nine runs and lots of ski lifts. Badger is an ideal place to learn to ski, and a ski school is available to enable that process. Free shuttle buses to Badger Pass are provided during the winter from lodging facilities in Yosemite Valley (and from other points on busy weekends). Call (209) 372-1446 for information about Badger Pass and the shuttle.

Several miles of both groomed and ungroomed trails for cross-country skiers also originate at Badger Pass. Tracks are laid out the Glacier Point Road all the way to Glacier Point, and skating lanes are also provided. Well-signed trails lead into the wilderness and out to the south rim of Yosemite Valley. The cross-country ski school at Badger offers classes, individualized instruction, and guided tours. Phone (209) 372-8444 for details.

A variety of services is available at the Badger Pass Ski Lodge. Snowboard and ski rentals (both downhill and cross-country), ski repair, child care, and food and beverage service are all offered. There's also a locker room and restrooms. The National Park Service staffs a ranger station primarily as a first aid facility in the A-frame building at Badger. The phone number is (209) 372- 0409.

Another popular cross-country ski area is Crane Flat located at the intersection of the Big Oak Flat and Tioga Roads, seventeen miles from Yosemite Valley. There are no services provided here, but the meadows and forests are full of trails for skiers and snowshoers both.

## Snowshoeing

You can showshoe on your own wherever there's adequate snow (at Badger Pass, Crane Flat, or the Mariposa Big Trees, for example), or enjoy a ranger-led showshoe walk where the snowshoes are provided. Walks are presented several days a week from in front of the A-frame at Badger Pass, and reservations are required. Check *Yosemite Today* or call (209) 372-0299.

*Merced River in winter, Yosemite Valley*

## Ice Skating

A large outdoor ice rink is operated daily in Yosemite Valley at Curry Village (weather permitting) from November through March. It features a smooth, refrigerated skating surface, rental skates, a warming hut with lockers, a fire pit, and snack stand. For hours and rates call (209) 372-8341.

## Snow Play

Provisions have been made for individuals and families with a passion for sledding, tobogganing, inner-tubing, and snow play generally. The designated area for these activities in Yosemite is at the Crane Flat Campground on the Big Oak Flat Road near its intersection with the Tioga Road. Another good snow play area is found just south of the park on Highway 41 at Goat Meadow in the Sierra National Forest. Supervise children well, and be careful. Many snow play related injuries occur every year.

## Camping

There are four campgrounds in Yosemite that are open for use during winter. In Yosemite Valley, both Upper Pines Campground (see page 35) and Sunnyside Walk-In Campground (see page 35) have been winterized. The Wawona Campground (see page 51) is the winter camping area south of the valley, and in the north end of the park, it's Hodgdon Meadow Campground (see page 68). Reservations are required for Upper Pines Campground (follow the procedure detailed on page 12), while all others are first-come, first-served.

## Backcountry Ski Huts

For the intrepid wilderness skier, two different huts are operated in Yosemite's backcountry. Nine miles from Badger Pass to the south of the Glacier Point Road is the Ostrander Lake Ski Hut. Set on the banks of a deeply frozen lake and below scenic Horse Ridge, the hut can accommodate up to 25 skiers overnight. There are beds with mattresses, cooking facilities, toilets, a wood stove, and water. Run by the Yosemite Association, the Ostrander Ski Hut is so popular that reservations are required. Call (209) 372-0740 for details, or write Ostrander, PO Box 545, Yosemite NP, CA 95389.

The second hut is located at Glacier Point and is reached by skiing the ten miles out from Badger Pass to the end of the Glacier Point Road. It is operated by DNC, which also requires reservations. Beds and meals are provided, and a guide will accompany you and do the cooking. To learn more about the Glacier Point Hut call (209) 372-8444.

## Junior Snow Rangers

The National Park Service offers a winter version of the Junior Ranger program (see page 23). By attending various ranger programs and completing a series of requirements, children can earn Junior Snow Ranger certificates and patches. Check the *Yosemite Today* or stop by a visitor center for details.

## The Bracebridge Dinner

Perhaps Yosemite's most long-standing winter tradition is the Bracebridge Dinner. A multi-course Christmas feast is presented at the Ahwahnee Hotel in the context of a colorful pageant based loosely on Washington Irving's Sketch Book account of a typical Yorkshire Christmas dinner in the manor of Squire Bracebridge. The music, costumes, food, and drama combine for an unforgettable experience. Tickets for the event (held multiple times) are in great demand, and reservations for the dinner are much sought after. For more information or to reserve tickets to Bracebridge, call (559) 252-4848. For the 2004 dinners, tickets were $300 per person (including taxes and gratuity), and reservations were accepted beginning February 2.

*Cross-country skiing*

## Where in the Park Can I Find....???

### Where can I find a public shower?

In Yosemite Valley, there are showers at Curry Village (open all year) and at Housekeeping Camp (closed in winter). The Tuolumne Meadows Lodge has public showers in summer only with very restricted hours. There are no public showers in Wawona. All showers require a fee.

### Where can I find a public laundromat?

The only park laundromat is at Housekeeping Camp in Yosemite Valley (open spring through autumn).

### Where can I find a post office?

In Yosemite Valley, the main post office is in Yosemite Village (near the Visitor Center), and there are branch offices at Curry Village (seasonal) and Yosemite Lodge (open all year). There is a year-round post office in the Wawona Store, and a summer-only post office in Tuolumne Meadows at the grocery store there.

### Where can I find an ATM (automated teller machine)?

In Yosemite Valley, there are ATMs in Yosemite Village inside the Village Store and to the south of the store at the Art Activity Center, at Yosemite Lodge inside the main registration area, and at Curry Village inside the gift/grocery store. In Wawona, the ATM is inside the Wawona Store, and at Tuolumne Meadows, it's inside the grocery store.

### Where can I find a babysitter?

Limited babysitting is available for registered guests at Yosemite Lodge and The Ahwahnee in Yosemite Valley. Call the front desk or see the concierge for additional information.

### Where can I find a dog kennel?

The only park kennel is in Yosemite Valley at the Yosemite Concession Services stables. Dogs must be gentle, over 10 pounds, and have proof of shots and a license. Call 372-8348 for more information.

### Where can I find a storage locker?

The only lockers in the park are in Yosemite Valley. They are coin-operated and located at Curry Village on the west side of the registration office.

### Where can I find a copy machine or a fax machine?

In Yosemite Valley, contact the front desk of Yosemite Lodge, Curry Village, or The Ahwahnee. A fee is charged for these services.

### Where can I find a good time?

If you're not enjoying yourself in Yosemite with all it has to offer, you need to see your therapist.

### Where can I find a cup of coffee?

In Yosemite Valley, visit the Food Court at Yosemite Lodge, Degnan's Deli in the village, and the Coffee Corner at Curry Village. There's also good coffee at The Ahwahnee dining room and bar.

*Steps on the Mist Trail*

## What Can I Do with my Children?

Though just being in Yosemite should be enough to keep young people occupied and engaged, there are lots of activities and programs that will enhance their visit to the park. During your stay, be sure to check the *Yosemite Today* newspaper for scheduled events that are specially designed for kids.

### Take a Hike
With just about every park locale offering flat to moderate walking, a family hike is a great way to burn youthful energy and to reach undeveloped, uncrowded spots with remarkable views and natural beauty. Take a picnic and make a day of it! See pages 30, 32, 45, 47, 59, 62, and 67 for hiking ideas.

### Enjoy a Bike Ride
The best park bicycle riding is in Yosemite Valley, which features miles of bike trails. Bring your own, or rent bicycles at Yosemite Lodge or Curry Village. See page 29 for details. Don't forget your helmets.

### Visit Happy Isles
The Nature Center at Happy Isles in Yosemite Valley is devoted to kids, with wildlife exhibits, nightlife display, and a number of other presentations. There are books for sale, and "Explorer Packs" on a variety of topics can be checked out. They include activities for children designed to help them learn more about the natural world they live in. See page 30.

### Help Them Become Junior Rangers
There are two self-guided "junior ranger" programs for kids in Yosemite. Children 3 through 6 can become "Little Cubs" and earn a button by completing the activities set out in *The Little Cub Handbook*, available at visitor centers throughout the park. *The Junior Ranger Handbook* is for those aged 7 to 13, and completion of the program allows them to become Junior Rangers and receive a certificate and patch. Any questions? Check with a ranger for more information.

### Explore the Indian Gallery and Garden
Within the Yosemite Museum in Yosemite Valley, a room has been dedicated to the culture of the local Native American people. Besides a number of educational displays, there is often someone demonstrating basketmaking or some other traditional art of the Miwok people. Behind the museum is a garden area that includes exhibits about the local Indians, and reproductions of several historic structures they might have used.

### Take in a Campfire Program
What better way to finish off a day than attending a traditional campfire program? During the summer, there are usually such programs offered by rangers in campgrounds throughout the park, and there is also a fee-based "Old-Fashioned Campfire" at Happy Isles in Yosemite Valley in spring, summer, and fall. Check the *Yosemite Today* newspaper for schedules.

## WINTER ACTIVITIES FOR KIDS

### Engage in Snow Play
Grab your sleds, toboggans, and inner tubes and head to the snow play areas at the Crane Flat Campground or just outside the South Entrance at Goat Meadow on Highway 41. Relatively gentle and clear slopes have been identified for hours of slipping and sliding.

### Go Skiing or Snowboarding
The ski area at Badger Pass is perfect for families, with nine runs, multiple lifts, and lessons offered by a first-rate ski school. Rental equipment is available for snowboarding and downhill and cross-country skiing. See page 20.

### Visit the Skating Rink
From November through March when weather allows, an outdoor ice rink operates at Curry Village beneath the shadow of Glacier Point. You can rent ice skates, and there's a warming hut, lockers, a fire pit, and a snack bar. The phone number is 372-8341.

### Snowshoe with a Ranger
Snowshoe walks are offered at Badger Pass by National Park Service rangers for adults and children 10 years and older. Rental snowshoes are available. Check the *Yosemite Today* newspaper for schedules.

# Yosemite Valley

**Roads**
- - - **Shuttle Bus Route**
**Autos prohibited**
**Trails**
Ⓟ Parking
Ⓡ Restroom
⋇ Vista Point
Ⅱ Food
⟙ Picnic Area
▲ Campground
Ⓐ Walk-in Campground
⑧ Shuttle Bus Stop

N

Eagle
Peak
Meadows

Yosemite Creek

Upper
Yosemite
Fall

Lower
Yosemite
Fall

Yosemite
Falls
Vista

Yosemite Falls Trail

Columbia
Point

Ⓡ
Ⓟ ⋇

6

Yosemite
Lodge

Ⅱ ⑧

8

THREE BROTHERS

▲ Eagle
Peak

Sunnyside
Ⓐ

Ⓟ
7

Swinging
Bridge ⟙
Ⓟ Ⓡ

Upper
Yosemite
Fall Vista

Horsetail
Fall

⟙ Sentinel
Beach

⟙

El Capitan

Northside Drive

To El Portal
& Merced

Cathedral
Rocks
Vista

El Capitan
Picnic
Area ⟙

Merced River

Southside Drive

El Capitan
Meadow

Cathedral
Beach ⟙

Three
Brothers
Vista

Bridalveil Creek

Taft Point Trail

Taft
Point

Pohono Trail

Yosemite Valley is truly the heart of the park. With its granite monoliths, towering waterfalls, and pastoral meadows, the valley is unique in the world for its remarkable scenery. Its seven square miles make up only a small fraction of the park's entire area, but 75 to 80 percent of the visitors to Yosemite spend their time there.

Not surprisingly, this popularity results in crowded conditions on popular weekends and during the summer. Campgrounds fill, concessioner accommodations become completely reserved, and day users clog valley roads and parking lots. Efforts have been made to reduce the congestion caused by such heavy use, and some improvements have resulted.

Among them are a one-way road system, the closure of roads to automobile traffic in the east end of the valley, development of an extensive network of bicycle paths, and the implementation of a shuttle bus system that links most developed areas in eastern Yosemite Valley.

## Can You Find the Visitor Center?

*"At Yosemite the visitor's center is almost impossible to find. By the time I found it I knew my way around and didn't need it anymore."* — Bill Bryson

Lots of visitors come to believe, after hours of searching, that the Yosemite Valley Visitor Center has been purposely hidden from them. In many national parks, the first place you are directed by prominent signs is the parking lot right smack in front of the Visitor Center. Not so in Yosemite Valley. Here you must either possess a doctorate in nuclear physics or have experience as a Green Beret to make your way to "Information Central."

It really is worth taking the time to find the Visitor Center because it's the ideal place to start your visit. There you will find an impressive orientation film program, interesting exhibits, information services provided by knowledgeable rangers, and a complete bookstore. Near the Visitor Center are an Indian Cultural Exhibit and Indian Garden, plus a Museum Gallery with new exhibits hung regularly.

Until 1971, a large paved parking lot at the center's front door was accessible to automobiles. But given the tremendous congestion that was occurring in the Yosemite Village area and the desire on the part of the National Park Service to begin to eliminate private vehicles from the valley, a decision was made to close the parking area and develop a pedestrian mall. The Visitor Center, for very good reasons, suddenly became unreachable by car.

But don't despair, you can still get to the Visitor Center by shuttle bus, on bicycle, or on foot. Here's how to manage it from selected valley locations.

### From Day Visitor Parking (Camp 6):
Park your car here and board one of the free "express" shuttle buses headed to the Yosemite Valley Visitor Center (bus stop #1). The bus stops in front of the Visitor Center (its only stop), then returns to the Day Visitor Parking area. If you'd rather walk, there's a map available at the information station there that will guide you. It's about a one-third mile hike.

### From the Pines Campgrounds:
Jump on a shuttle bus at the stop nearest to you (bus stops #15, #16, and #21 are all close), and disembark at Yosemite

Village (bus stop #2). The Visitor Center is 200 yards to the west up the mall.

**From Housekeeping Camp:** The shuttle bus stops right in front of the entrance to the camp {bus stop #13). Take it and get off at Yosemite Village (bus stop #2). Walk 200 yards to the west up the pedestrian mall to the Visitor Center.

**From the Ahwahnee Hotel:** It's about a fifteen minute walk along the Ahwahnee Meadow and past the Church Bowl to the Visitor Center. Or take the free shuttle bus from in front of the hotel (bus stop #3) and get off at the Visitor Center (bus stop #5).

**From Yosemite Lodge:** Catch the free shuttle bus in front of the lodge registration area (bus stop #8). It will drop you off a few yards from the Visitor Center's front door (bus stop #9). The walk from Yosemite Lodge to the Visitor Center is less than a mile, it's flat and easy, and affords lots of good views along the way.

**From the Parking Area behind the Village Store:** Walk around or through the Village Store to the pedestrian mall on the other side of it. Turn to your right and walk approximately 200 yards up the mall to the Visitor Center.

These directions should make it clear that the key to finding the Visitor Center is locating the Yosemite Village pedestrian mall. The center is located at the mall's west end. If you're on your bicycle, bike trails are well marked, and signs will direct you to Yosemite Village and the Visitor Center.

### Free Shuttle Bus Rides

The easiest way to get around in Yosemite Valley (and to get out of your car and avoid traffic) is to ride, free of charge, the Yosemite Valley shuttle bus system. With stops at just about all locations in the eastern end of the valley, the buses run every ten minutes or so (somewhat less frequently in the winter) and access areas such as Happy Isles and Mirror Lake that are closed to private automobiles. All the shuttle bus stops are indicated on the map below. In winter, shuttle service is discontinued to several stops.

**Q:** Where was the original Visitor Center (park headquarters) located in Yosemite Valley?

**A:** In old Yosemite Village, across from the present-day Yosemite Chapel just west of Sentinel Bridge.

## Best Bets in Yosemite Valley

**The view from Glacier Point.** From the railing at Glacier Point, you are lord (or lady) of all the Yosemite you survey. The view is unforgettable. See page 39.

**John Muir in person.** Noted actor Lee Stetson regularly portrays John Muir in dramatic presentations in Yosemite Valley. It's Yosemite Theater at its best. See page 31.

**A browse through The Ansel Adams Gallery.** This classy shop has been a leading Yosemite establishment since 1902. If you're a photographer, consider this your headquarters in the park. See page 22.

**The hike to Vernal Fall.** An amazingly popular trip, but for good reason. The walk is essential Yosemite: rock, light, and water at their most spectacular. See page 33.

**A seat at Bracebridge Dinner.** This lavish Christmas pageant is held annually at the Ahwahnee Hotel and features much delicious food, seasonal music, elaborate costumes, and festive decorations. See page 21.

**Breakfast at The Ahwahnee.** It's a delight anytime of the year to start your day with a casual yet luxurious breakfast in The Ahwahnee's grand dining room. See page 37.

**The panorama from Tunnel View.** This classic Yosemite viewpoint never ceases to take one's breath. From this spot the valley's geologic origin couldn't be more evident. See page 39.

**A visit to the Visitor Center Bookstore.** Nowhere else in the universe has such a complete collection of books and other materials related to Yosemite and the Sierra Nevada been assembled in one place. See page 26.

**Lower Yosemite Fall in springtime.** When the snows of the Yosemite high country begin to thaw, the results are a revitalized Yosemite Falls. Liquid thunder! See page 32.

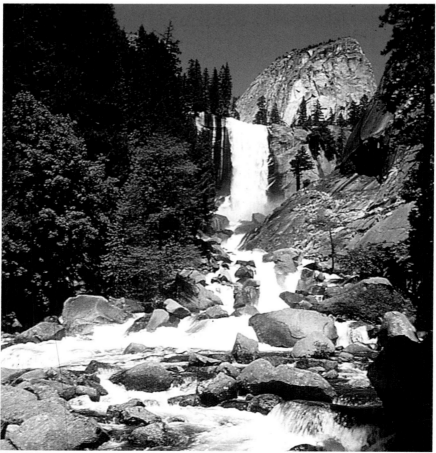

*Vernal Fall*

## Activities in the Valley

Once you have spent some time at the Visitor Center (page 26), there are unlimited possibilities for visitor enjoyment. Most of them involve seeing and learning about the amazing sights that Yosemite Valley has to offer.

### Enjoy an Interpretive Program

Throughout the year, park interpretive rangers and others present a wide variety of programs, walks, demonstrations, campfires, slideshows, films, and talks. There is usually no charge for these activities, which occasionally do require reservations. Consult the *Yosemite Today* for the daily schedule for these programs.

### Visit Yosemite Valley's Eastern End

The free shuttle bus route takes visitors to the area of Yosemite Valley that is no longer accessible by private automobile. Such locations as Happy Isles (the trailhead for the hikes to Vernal and Nevada Falls and Half Dome) and Mirror Lake can only be reached by the shuttle bus or on bicycle and foot. Excellent views of many landmarks including Glacier Point, Half Dome, Tenaya Canyon, and Washington Column are afforded from stops along the way. This section of the shuttle bus route is closed in winter.

### Make a Circle Tour of the Entire Valley

To reach much of Yosemite Valley to the west of Yosemite Village you must still use your car. Many of the park's most famous spots such as El Capitan, Bridalveil Fall, Tunnel View, Cathedral Rocks, and Sentinel Rock are in west valley locations. At least two resources are available for a "self-guided" circle tour. If you've got a CD player in your car, try the *Yosemite Valley Tour – A Yosemite Audio Guide* by Bob Roney.

This audio tour is available for sale at the Visitor Center and other park stores, and is a comprehensive look at all aspects of the valley – from geology to Native Americans to history to plants and animals. The sixty-minute CD provides explicit directions to the ten stops on the tour that will take you from 2 to 4 hours.

An alternative is to use *The Yosemite Road Guide,* a well-written book that is keyed to roadside markers throughout Yosemite Valley and the rest of the park. You must develop your own route using the guide, but it's packed with interesting information and facts that will enhance your tour.

If you would rather be free of your car and not drive, DNC offers a two-hour guided tour in an open-air tram that visits most of the picturesque spots in Yosemite Valley. Check at the front desks of the various lodging facilities or behind the Village Store for tour details and prices.

### Take a Bicycle Ride

Whether you've brought your bicycle or not, you can still see Yosemite Valley on two wheels. Bicycle rentals (with helmet) can be arranged all year at Yosemite Lodge (372-1208) and summer only at Curry Village (372-8319). More than eight miles of paved bicycle paths separate bicycle traffic from autos, and bicycling is especially good on the closed sections of roadway in the valley's east end.

Try to avoid bicycling on busy valley roads that are often flooded with automobiles. As a rule, distracted, sight-seeing drivers are not particularly attentive to bicyclists. Apart from that, there are some fairly strict rules for bicycle use in the valley:

- Bicyclists should stay on paved bike paths and highways.
- No riding on trails and into meadows. Erosion and vegetation damage will result otherwise.
- Mountain and all terrain bicycles are permitted, but not allowed on unpaved surfaces in Yosemite Valley. Check at the Visitor Center for appropriate mountain bike routes.
- Ride to the right in single file.

### Catch a Fish

There are lots of trout in Yosemite Valley, but the Merced River is heavily fished. Stocking of trout is no longer done, and resident lunkers have developed a wariness of people and their multifarious fishing devices. Nevertheless, nice fish are caught every season by anglers of every skill level.

Fishing in Yosemite is allowed in streams and rivers from the last Saturday in April to November 15. Fishing is allowed year-round in park lakes and reservoirs. On the

Merced River in Yosemite Valley, only catch-and-release fishing is allowed for rainbow trout. No natural or organic bait may be used, only artificial lures and flies with barbless hooks. The limit is 5 per day with 10 in possession. California fishing licenses are required (16 years and over) and may be purchased at the Village Sports Shop and at the Wawona Store.

On the Merced River just outside the park between the boundary and downstream to the Foresta Bridge, fishing is allowed all year but only to persons using artificial lures with barbless hooks, with a minimum size limit of 12 inches total length and a maximum daily bag limit of 2. Consult the California Fish and Game Regulations for further Yosemite fishing rules.

### Paint a Picture

Free outdoor art classes are available during most parts of the year at the Yosemite Art Center. Artists working in many different media offer hands-on learning experiences to interested students regardless of skill level. Located on the Village Mall south of the Village Store near Shuttle Stop #2, the Yosemite Art Center is co-sponsored by the National Park Service, the Yosemite Association, and DNC Parks & Resorts at Yosemite. Class sessions are four hours in length and are scheduled from early spring through October, and during holiday periods.

### Ride 'Em Cowboy

Horseback rides are offered (for those with hardened backsides) by DNC Parks & Resorts at Yosemite from their stables in the east end of Yosemite Valley (bus stop #18). Guided trips in two-hour, half-day, and full-day lengths are given to such destinations as Nevada Fall and Glacier Point. For reservations and information call 372-8348 between 7:30 a.m. and 5 p.m.

### Get Your Head Wet

If you'd like to swim, the Merced River provides miles of beaches and numerous refreshing swimming holes during the summer months (it's too cold and fast-flowing in the spring). Or try out Mirror Lake and Tenaya Creek. If you must swim in a heated pool, in summer there's one at Yosemite Lodge and another at Curry Village. A small pool is available for guests only at the Ahwahnee Hotel.

### Indulge the Kids

The Nature Center at Happy Isles (near Shuttle Stop #16) is a great spot for parents and their children, open from early spring until October (check the *Yosemite Today*). You can purchase workbooks for the Junior Ranger and Little Cub programs, and there are exhibits of park animals, a children's corner, a night display, and much more. Kids can check out, free of charge, an "Explorer Pack" – a convenient-to-carry daypack filled with guide books and activities for the whole family. There are packs available on different topics including "Small Wonders," "Tree Trivia," and "Rocking in Yosemite."

### Go for a Hike

There's a price to be paid for Yosemite Valley's towering cliffs and sheer walls. Practically every hike leading out of Yosemite Valley is straight up and strenuous! But the valley floor offers many enjoyable walks over flat terrain, and no matter what your hiking ability, you can find a trail to suit you. Several Yosemite Valley floor trails are wheelchair accessible.

When you hike be sure to wear sturdy, comfortable shoes and clothes that allow freedom of movement. Carry a flashlight and raingear. Rain (or snow) is a possibility in every season. Don't forget plenty of water (drinking from streams and rivers is not advised), and lunch and snacks. Dogs on leash are allowed on trails on the floor of Yosemite Valley, but nowhere else.

## Take in the Yosemite Theater

Throughout the year, dramatic and musical performances are offered by the Yosemite Theater program. Designed to supplement the interpretive activities of the NPS, Yosemite Theater is sponsored by DNC Parks & Resorts at Yosemite. Modest fees are charged for the various presentations. Best known of the theater programs are Lee Stetson's one-man stage productions in which he portrays John Muir. There's a program for every taste including musical campfire programs and slide and film presentations. Tickets for the performances may be purchased at the door, or check at DNC activities desks.

## Hear a Lecture

Each summer the Sierra Club operates the LeConte Memorial Lodge, an educational center and library located across from Housekeeping Camp at shuttle bus stop #12. The lodge was built by the Club in 1903 in honor of Joseph LeConte, eminent University of California geologist. Berkeley architect John White designed the Tudor-style, rough-hewn granite building. Most evenings, special lectures are presented here free of charge to interested visitors and Sierra Club members. Consult the *Yosemite Today* or visit the LeConte Lodge for a schedule.

## Saunter in the Cemetery

Fascinating insights into Yosemite's history can be gained from a visit to the Yosemite Cemetery located across the street just west of the Yosemite Museum. Several significant figures from the park's past are buried here including a number of Native Americans. First laid out in the 1870s, the cemetery houses the graves of such persons as James Mason Hutchings, Galen Clark, James Lamon, Sally Ann Castagnetto, Suzie Sam, and Lucy Brown. An informative publication entitled *Guide to the Yosemite Valley Cemetery* is on sale at the Visitor Center. If you do visit the cemetery, remember that it is a sacred place for many and that proper respect should be shown.

## Wheelchair Accessibility

Many programs, facilities, and trails in Yosemite Valley (and throughout the park) are suitable for visitors in wheelchairs, with assistance. Information on accessible park programs, facilities, and trails can be found in the *Yosemite Magazine* or at park entrance and information stations.

**Q:** How many rangers does it take to change a light bulb?

**A:** None. Rangers aren't afraid of the dark.

## Visit the Wilderness Center

Located in the small building between The Ansel Adams Gallery and the post office, the Wilderness Center offers a number of informative displays, a great relief map of the entire park, information on planning your own trip into the wilderness, and maps, guidebooks, and selected backpacking items. It's also the place to pick up wilderness permits, make wilderness reservations (see page 16), and rent bear-resistant food canisters.

## Pack a Picnic

There are a number of fine spots for a picnic in Yosemite Valley. In the eastern end of the valley, ride the shuttle bus to Happy Isles or take the walk to Mirror Lake. To the west try El Capitan picnic area (on the right side of Northside Drive about two miles west of Yosemite Lodge), Bridalveil Fall parking area (intersection of the Wawona Road and Southside Drive), Cathedral picnic area (on the left side of Southside Drive just past the El Cap crossover), Sentinel Beach picnic area (on the left a mile or so further along Southside Drive), or Swinging Bridge picnic area (less than half a mile further on the left). See the map on page 24-25 for locations.

## Enjoy an Outdoor Adventure

Throughout the year, the Yosemite Association presents a series of outdoor seminars in Yosemite Valley and at other park locations. Some of the courses, covering such topics as botany, geology, natural history, photography, art, and backpacking, are offered for college credit. Programs have been designed for all levels of experience and for every type of Yosemite user. The instructional staff is excellent. For a catalog of classes or more information call (209) 379-2321, visit www.yosemite.org, or write: Outdoor Adventures, Box 230, El Portal, CA 95318.

**Q:** Where did the Mariposa Battalion camp on their first ever visit to Yosemite Valley in 1851?

**A:** In Bridalveil Meadow. There's a plaque commemorating this event on the edge of the meadow near the Merced River.

## Three Easy Hikes on the Valley Floor

**Mirror Lake.** Take the free shuttle bus to the Mirror Lake Junction (bus stop #17). During the winter you'll have to walk from the Pines Campgrounds (bus stop #19). From this point it's a relaxing half-mile saunter over pavement to Mirror Lake. The trail beyond is also gentle as it follows Tenaya Creek eastward and then circles back. Walking up Tenaya Creek adds about 3 miles to the total distance. Views of Half Dome, Mt. Watkins, and Basket Dome are superb.

**Vernal Fall Bridge.** This special vantage point is reached from Happy Isles (stop #16 on the free shuttle bus route). You'll need to walk from Curry Village during the winter when the shuttles don't run this way. Undoubtedly the most popular and busiest hike in Yosemite (you'll be elbow to elbow with lots of other people), the Mist Trail leads seven-tenths of a mile to a bridge that allows a breathtaking view of Vernal Fall. The trail, while paved with asphalt, is not as easy as the other two hikes listed here.

There is a moderate slope most of the way to the bridge, and a few ups and downs. But its definitely worth the effort. If you're a strong hiker and still feeling hardy, the remaining hike to the top of the fall is about a half-mile. Be warned, however, that it's all straight uphill over a very steep trail and a large number of granite steps. It's called the Mist Trail because it leads along the right flank of Vernal Fall, which, particularly in spring, blows heavy mist over trail and hiker alike.

**Lower Yosemite Fall.** Walk, drive, bicycle, or ride the shuttle bus to the Lower Yosemite Fall parking area near Yosemite Lodge (bus stop #6). It's no more than a quarter-mile to the base of the lower fall and its boisterous, watery display (at least most of the year). This, too, is a very popular excursion. If you continue over the bridge and follow the trail, you will loop back to the parking area in less than a half-mile. On full-moon nights in April and May, take this walk and watch for beautiful "moon bows" in the lower fall—a phenomenon first written about by John Muir.

**Note:** The floor of Yosemite Valley is crisscrossed with many trails, and paths hug the base of both the north and south valley walls. From about any point, there's good hiking. Wherever you walk, be sure it's not on one of the main roadways. Get out of your car and explore some of Yosemite's less-developed locales. You'll be amply rewarded for your effort.

### Further Reading

*Easy Day Hikes in Yosemite* by Deborah Durkee. Yosemite NP: Yosemite Association, 2000.

*Map & Guide to Yosemite Valley* by Dean Shenk. San Francisco: Rufus Graphics, 2001.

*The Waterfalls of Yosemite* by Steven P. Medley. Yosemite NP: Yosemite Association, 1999.

## Four Classic Routes to Yosemite Valley's Rim

Each of the major trails to the valley rim is very strenuous and requires an uphill hike of at least 3.5 miles over tens of switchbacks. Be sure you possess the requisite time, energy, and physical condition before you set off on any of these hikes.

**1. Yosemite Falls Trail.** This climb up the sheer north wall pays off with remarkable perspectives on both the falls and Yosemite Valley generally. The trail leaves from behind Sunnyside Campground across from Yosemite Lodge. The 3.6-mile route gains 2,700 feet in elevation as it passes Columbia Point, the top of Lower Yosemite Fall, and finally leads to the brink of Upper Yosemite Fall. When you reach the top, head back south toward the rim and find the walk down to the pipe railings. At this lookout, water leaps from the rock and braids itself into impressive patterns below you. Allow 6 to 8 hours for the round trip. Strong hikers should consider continuing on to Yosemite Point or Eagle Peak (see page 39).

**2. The Four-Mile Trail to Glacier Point.** Perhaps most disappointing to hikers on this route is that the Four-Mile Trail is almost 5 miles long (maybe somebody rounded off a little too liberally). It's also an awful lot of work carrying yourself up 3,200 feet only to be greeted by automobiles, lots of people, and a snack bar at your destination. But the views from Glacier Point are sensational and all the more satisfying for the exertion. The trailhead is below Sentinel Rock on Southside Drive about a mile from Yosemite Village at road marker V18. To drive to it you must make a loop on the valley's one-way road system, crossing over at El Capitan (watch for signs returning you to Yosemite Village). One of the earliest trails built in the valley, it is generally cooler than other routes to the rim given its location below and along the south wall. This hike requires from 6 to 8 hours up and back.

**3. Tenaya Zigzags/Snow Creek Trail.** This is a less-used 3.5-mile route to the rim that actually originates in Tenaya Canyon, just east of Mirror Lake about 2.5 miles from shuttle stop #17. It affords stunning views of the canyon including those of Clouds Rest and Quarter Dome, and directly across from you as you ascend, of Half Dome. Once you've hiked the 108 switchbacks to the rim, the closest promontory is North Dome, which is another 3 miles (see page 39). If North Dome is your destination, allow 8 to 10 hours round trip. The trailhead is Mirror Lake, reached by taking a shuttle bus to the Mirror Lake junction (bus stop #17) and hiking a half-mile to the east. From the lake the trail takes off to the north of the lake up the

canyon for a mile and a half, then turns left up the cliff.

**4. Vernal and Nevada Falls Trails.** The walk to Vernal Fall over the Mist Trail is covered in the "Easy Hikes" section (page 32), but the trail continues on to Nevada Fall above. Describing the route is a bit difficult, because there are two different segments leading to the same place—one primarily for horses and one exclusively for people. The horse trail takes off just past the Vernal Fall Bridge and is less steep, though longer (3.5 miles to Nevada Fall). The Mist Trail (foot traffic only) continues on past the top of Vernal Fall about a mile and a half over switchbacks to the rim. Ascending a gully to its left, hikers are treated to the world-famous profile view of Nevada Fall. From the top of the fall, trails lead to Little Yosemite Valley and Half Dome, and to Glacier Point over the Panorama Trail. Depart from Happy Isles (bus stop #16) and give yourself 6 to 8 hours for the round trip.

*Mist Trail*

**Half Dome: The Hike.** For many the summit of Half Dome represents a hiking challenge they can't resist. For all its allure, the trip is long (about 17 miles round trip), steep (4,900 feet of elevation gain), and physically demanding. It's rewarding, too, particularly the incredible views both along the way and at the top. The last 200 yards up the back of the dome require the use of steel-cable handrails and will really make your adrenal gland active. If it sounds like too much of a grunt for one day, consider spending the night in Little Yosemite Valley (you'll need a wilderness permit) and make the ascent when you're fresh the next morning. This busy trail (someone estimated that about 700 people scale Half Dome daily during the summer) begins from Happy Isles (bus stop #16). Allow 10 to 12 hours minimum for the round trip.

**Q:** What was the preferred route of the Yosemite Indians to the north rim of Yosemite Valley?

**A:** They regularly used what we now call Indian Canyon, but no trail is maintained any longer up this very steep ravine.

## Valley Camping

*Yosemite Valley for a home or camp,*
*the Grand Canyon for a spectacle.*
—John Burroughs

There are about 415 campsites in Yosemite Valley, most of them on the NPRS reservation system year-round. Despite the fact that many of the campgrounds are practically void of vegetation and that campers are closely packed, these campsites are immensely popular. After all, it's Yosemite Valley.

It was in response to this popularity that the strictly-structured reservation system was developed. While the need to reserve in advance does discourage spontaneity and acting on impulse, it allows visitors coming from all over the US and the rest of the world to expect, with some certainty, that they will find a place to camp when they arrive. From all appearances and reports, the system works well.

As indicated above, the campground reservation system is administered by NPRS, which has some fairly exact requirements. See page 12 for information on making an NPRS reservation.

For campers without reservations who find themselves in Yosemite Valley, there is an NPRS office at the north side of the parking area at Curry Village. Occasionally campsites become available due to cancellation, but to obtain one of them requires standing in line, sometimes for long periods of time. These sites are very limited and nearly impossible to obtain. You must put your name on a waiting list at the Curry Village campground reservation office as early in the day as possible.

### Camping Regulations

**Camping Limits:** From May 1 through September 15, there is a seven-day camping limit in the valley. It extends to 30 days between September 16 and April 30. Thirty total camping days per calendar year are permitted in the park (the "no homsteading" rule). A maximum of six people is allowed in each campsite.

**Check Out Time:** Campsites must be vacated by 10 a.m. on the day of departure. Check-in time is also 10 a.m., and sites may not be occupied before that time.

**Bears:** Yosemite Valley and other park locations provide excellent bear habitat. Bears are attracted by the same foods many campers enjoy—marshmallows, hot dogs, watermelon, etc. You are foolish if you do not store your food properly in your campsite (it's also a federal law). All of the valley campgrounds feature bear-proof food lockers measuring 45"w x 18"h x 34"d

that are very effective. Keep your bear locker latched and secured with its clips at all times. Food is not allowed in any parked vehicle after dark. Remove all trash from your campsite and place it in animal-resistant trash cans or dumpsters.

**Pets:** You may camp with your pets only in designated campgrounds. Be sure to inform NPRS when you make your reservation that you'll be bringing Fido or Garfield. Pets must be on leashes (no longer than six feet) at all times, should never be left unattended, and are not permitted on trails off the floor of Yosemite Valley.

**Hook-Ups:** There are no recreational vehicle utility hookups in the park. Electrical extension cords may not be connected to campground restroom outlets. Sneaky, but no cigar.

**Fires and Firewood:** Collection of firewood of any kind (including dead and down wood) in Yosemite Valley is strictly prohibited. This regulation is the first step towards eliminating campfires that have contributed significantly to serious air quality problems in the valley. (It's also aimed at making people smell less smokey.) Campfires are permitted only between 5 p.m. and 10 p.m. At this time, firewood may still be purchased from the concessioner. Please use established fire rings and grates, and start your campfire with newspaper, not pine needles or cones. Use of chain saws is not permitted in the park.

**Vehicle Parking:** Only two vehicles are allowed per site. All of your vehicles including tent and utility trailers must be parked on the parking pads. You can't just drive into your campsite. If you have more than two vehicles, you must park any extras outside the campground. The maximum length for recreational vehicles is 40 feet.

**Dump Stations:** No wastewater of any kind should be drained onto the ground. That's gross. Use utility drains at campground restrooms for dishwater and other gray water. Use the dump station at Upper Pines Campground for RV and other septic tanks.

**Quiet Hours:** Campers are expected to maintain quiet between 10 p.m. and 6 a.m. Quiet generators may be used sparingly during the daytime. Or not at all if I'm camped next to you.

**Showers:** Try to stay clean during your visit. Unfortunately, there are no shower facilities in any park campgrounds. In Yosemite Valley, showers are available for a fee at Curry Village and at Housekeeping Camp.

**Laundry:** There is a public laundromat at Housekeeping Camp.

## Valley Campgrounds

The following campgrounds are located at an elevation of 4,000 feet in the eastern end of Yosemite Valley. Most require NPRS reservations (see page 12) and have a nightly fee of $18 per site (unless otherwise indicated). Some creative person decided to include "pines" in the name of practically every valley campground, so be sure to take note of the location you've been assigned or you may spend hours trying to find your way home. As dates of operation are subject to variation, check with NPRS or the NPS for details.

**North Pines:** This set of 84 campsites is located adjacent to the stables and next to the Merced River. Both recreational vehicles and tents are accommodated here between April and September. Some pets allowed. NPRS reservations required.

**Upper Pines:** The easternmost campground and the largest in Yosemite Valley, Upper Pines is closest to Happy Isles and the trail to Vernal and Nevada Falls. There are 238 sites here, and some pets are permitted. Both RVs and tents are welcome, and a sanitary dump station is available. Open all year. NPRS reservations required.

**Lower Pines:** Across the river from North Pines with several campsites near the banks of the Merced. The 60 campsites are available for both recreational vehicle users and traditional tent campers. Open March to October. Some pets are allowed. NPRS reservations required.

**Sunnyside Walk-in:** This campground is primarily for climbers and backpackers; traditional family campers would feel out of place here. Climbing headquarters for Yosemite Valley, Sunnyside attracts mountaineers from all over the world. It's located across from Yosemite Lodge on Northside Drive. Parking spaces are provided outside the camping area, and users must carry their equipment and food to their sites. The 35 campsites are communal in nature (six campers are assigned to each); the nightly fee is $5 per person. Operated on a first-come, first-served basis, Sunnyside is not on the NPRS system. Be sure to arrive early because the campground fills up by mid-morning practically every day of the summer. These campsites are not wheelchair accessible. Open for walk-in campers all year round; no pets are allowed.

**Backpacker Walk-in:** Designed for backpackers (be prepared to show your wilderness permit), bicyclists, and bus passengers, this area of 25 sites has no parking area. All access is by foot and there is a one-night maximum stay. Users should check in at North Pines Campground, where a ranger will provide directions to the area. Open from April to October in a typical year. Campers are charged $5 per person per night on a first-come, first-served basis (NPRS procedures do not apply). No pets are allowed.

**Group Campground:** Special campsites are available for organized groups in Yosemite Valley by prior arrangement; reservations can be made through NPRS starting five months in advance. The fee is $50 per site for no fewer than 13 and no more than 30 people. Parking is provided for up to five vehicles per group, and all equipment and gear must be carried to the campground. For information and reservations contact NPRS at the address on page 12 or visit the NPRS online site at www.reservations.nps.gov. The group campground is not wheelchair accessible and no pets are allowed.

### Campfire Limits

From May 1 through October 15, campfires are permitted only between 5 p.m. and 10 p.m. in Yosemite Valley. This measure was implemented to protect the air quality in Yosemite National Park. You should plan to bring your own firewood (wood gathering is not permitted in Yosemite Valley), or buy firewood at one of the valley stores.

## Gas Food & Lodging

### Gas

There are no longer any service stations in Yosemite Valley and gas is not available. The nearest gas to be pumped is in El Portal on Highway 140 (13 miles). There are also stations at Crane Flat on the Big Oak Flat Road (15 miles), and in Wawona on the Wawona Road (27 miles). Plan ahead and be sure you have plenty of gas before you drive into the valley.

A repair garage is open all year behind the Yosemite Village Store. A towing service is available 24 hours a day by calling 372-8390.

### Food: Restaurants

*Though the cuisine is strictly American and waits can be considerable during the summer, there are plenty of places to eat in Yosemite Valley. The following is a location-by-location listing of valley eating establishments. Check the* Yosemite Today *for hours of operation.*

### Yosemite Lodge

**Food Court:** Open for breakfast, lunch, and dinner the year round. Quick and perfect for families. Many different choices, plus a good coffee bar. Inexpensive.*

**The Mountain Room:** Offering dinner only, daily from spring to fall, and on weekends and holidays in winter. This is Yosemite's "steak house," with other entrees including salmon and pasta. The remodeled facility is very impressive, and the room offers remarkable views of the Yosemite Falls area from many tables. And it's one of the only places to dine out-of-doors in the summer. Open from 5:30 to 8:30 p.m. Moderate to expensive.

**The Mountain Room Bar & Lounge:** Besides beer, wine, and cocktails, this facility offers a la carte continental breakfast, and lunch featuring gourmet coffee, sandwiches, salads, cold appetizer plates, and yogurt. Hours vary, but it's usually open from 6:30 a.m. to 10 p.m. Inexpensive to moderate.

### Yosemite Village

**Degnan's Deli:** Open year round for sandwiches, snacks, salads, and picnic items. They will build a sandwich to your specifications, and you can piece together a nice lunch basket. There's limited outdoor seating so plan on making yours a moveable feast. Inexpensive to moderate.

**Degnan's Fast Food & Ice Cream:** Lunch and dinner selections, year around. Fare includes hamburgers, chicken, frozen yogurt, and ice cream. Limited indoor seating, but a fairly large patio. Inexpensive.

**The Loft:** Serving lunch and dinner, spring to fall. Located upstairs at the east end of the Degnan's building, The Loft offers pizza, salads, and appetizers from a cafeteria-style line, with plenty of indoor seating. Moderate.

**The Village Grill:** Fast food breakfasts, lunches, and dinners, spring to fall. Patterned roughly on a MacDonald's menu (look for the Royal Arches?), offerings include burgers, chicken strips, sandwiches, shakes, and fries, with a morning menu of breakfast sandwiches and entrees. Located next to the Village Store with outdoor seating only. Inexpensive.

### Curry Village

**Pavilion Buffet:** For breakfast and dinner spring to fall. Breakfast items include yogurt, cereal, fruit, baked goods, and hot entrees. For dinner, there's soup, salad, pasta, hot entrees, stir-fry, taco bar, and desserts. A family favorite with inexpensive to moderate prices.

**Hamburger Stand:** Open spring to fall, this fast food outlet has about the same offerings as the Village Grill. Hamburgers, chicken, fish sandwiches, chicken nuggets, salad, and soft drinks to go for consumption on the deck outside. Inexpensive.

**Pizza & Bar:** Open daily from spring to fall, this facility offers pizza and salad from 4:30 p.m. to 10 p.m. on weekdays, and from noon to 10 p.m. on weekends. Tables are outdoors on the deck. Inexpensive to moderate.

**Taqueria:** Open daily from spring to fall, this new facility offers Mexican food from 11 a.m. to 5 p.m. Early and late in the season it only operates on weekends. Inexpensive to moderate.

**Coffee Corner:** For the caffeine-deprived; here you can find fresh ground coffees, espressos, lattes, cappuccinos, fruit, baked goods, and boxed lunches. Located within the Curry Pavilion. Inexpensive.

**Ice Cream:** Open spring to fall, this small outlet offers sweet treats. It's located inside the Curry Pavilion at the Coffee Corner. Inexpensive.

---

* Inexpensive: dinner for one adult might cost up to $10. Moderate: dinner for one adult might cost from $10 to $20. Expensive: dinner for one adult might cost over $20.

The Ahwahnee

## The Ahwahnee
### The Ahwahnee Dining Room:
Breakfast, lunch, and dinner, year round. This regal dining room is a true delight. It's a joy to behold with its beamed ceilings and impressive chandeliers. Perhaps breakfast is the most enjoyable meal here; casual attire is allowed and one experiences a feeling of relaxation and elegance as daylight filters through the massive windows. Dinner is the traditional, formal meal at The Ahwahnee (though the views are obscured by darkness). Men must wear jackets with ties preferred, and reservations are suggested. Call 372-1489. Moderate to expensive.

**The Ahwahnee Bar:** Light fare and appetizers are served in the bar from noon to 10 p.m daily. Moderate.

## Food: Groceries
*Yosemite Valley contains four outlets for groceries and camp supplies. They are open year round with the exception of the Housekeeping Camp Store which closes in winter. Check the* Yosemite Today *for hours of operation, or call the indicated phone number.*

**Village Store:** If you can't find it anywhere else in Yosemite Valley, come here. Of particular note are the butcher shop and the fresh produce. Located at the east end of the Village Mall at bus stop #2. Open from 8 a.m. to 9 p.m. (and sometimes later). Phone 372-1253.

**Degnan's Delicatessen:** Included in the restaurant listings above, Degnan's Deli also has a decent selection of foodstuffs for picknicking and snacks. West of the Village Store and next to the U.S. Post Office on the mall. Open from 8 a.m. to 6 p.m. Phone 372-8454.

**Curry Village Camp Store:** A general store with convenience items and gifts. Located in the Pavilion building next to the Hamburger deck at Curry Village. Open from 8 a.m. to 7 p.m. Phone 372-8325.

**Housekeeping Camp Store:** This is a convenience store catering to campers. It's open from spring to fall only, usually between 8 a.m. and 6 p.m. (and sometimes later). Located at Housekeeping Camp near shuttle bus stop #12. Phone 372-8353.

## Lodging
*The following is a list of lodging facilities, ranging from rustic to luxurious, existing in Yosemite Valley. Quoted rates are approximate only, based on double occupancy, vary with the seasons, and are subject to change. Some rates are lower in winter. Some room rates were scheduled to be reviewed in April, 2004. To make reservations, see page 11.*

## Yosemite Lodge
Open all year, the lodge offers two types of accommodations: there are 229 lodge rooms ($156 plus tax in season) and 19 standard rooms ($109 plus tax in season). Special value-season rates (both weekend and mid-week) are available between November 1 and March 15. Yosemite Lodge is preferred to Curry Village in winter because of its warmer location. The Lodge is situated near and offers pleasant views of Yosemite Falls and the Merced River.

Besides the restaurants listed above, the following are available at Yosemite Lodge: gift shops, cocktail lounge, tour/activities desk, post office, outdoor amphitheater, swimming pool, bicycle rentals, and free shuttle service to various locations in the park.

Curry Village

## Curry Village
Open from spring to fall and on holidays and weekends in winter. Originally designed to provide an economical lodging alternative in Yosemite Valley, Curry Village still features the least expensive accommodations. They are of four types: standard motel rooms with bath ($109 plus tax in season), cabins with bath ($87 plus tax in season), cabins without bath ($80 plus tax in season), and canvas tent cabins without bath ($64 plus tax in season). Special value-season rates (both weekend and mid-week) are available between November 1 and March 15. All cabins without bath utilize communal bathrooms.

Curry Village is cooler in summer than other valley locations and is known for its informality. Nearby attractions are Happy Isles, the campgrounds, and the riding stables.

Other amenities include gift shops, showers, a mountaineering shop, a climbing school, swimming pool, an outdoor amphitheater, tour/activities desk, free shuttle service to various locations in the park, and bicycle and raft rentals, plus an ice rink in winter.

### The Ahwahnee

Ansel Adams called The Ahwahnee "one of the world's distinctive resort hotels." Open year-round, this grand and imposing hotel is definitely at the luxury end of the Yosemite lodging spectrum. Besides its regular rooms in the main building, The Ahwahnee features several cottages on the grounds. Rooms and cottages all have bathrooms and rent for $371 plus tax per night. Parlor rooms are $447 plus tax per night.

The hotel's Great Lounge is a study in high style (afternoon tea offers a relaxing respite), and the dining room (see page 37) is without parallel as an elegant setting for a meal. Located below the Royal Arches, The Ahwahnee offers fine views of Glacier Point and the valley's south wall.

Other guest services available at The Ahwahnee are gift shops, a cocktail lounge, and a swimming pool for guests of the hotel only.

### Housekeeping Camp

The experience at Housekeeping Camp is somewhere between camping out and staying in a rustic cabin. Guests are provided a developed "campsite" that features a covered shelter, a cooking and dining area, cots, a table, and a fire ring. You must bring your own linen (or sleeping bags) and cookware. Call it luxury camping, if you prefer, which differs from staying in a Curry Village tent cabin because you are able to prepare your own meals. Each housekeeping unit rents for $64 plus tax (plus $5 per each person over 4), and the camp is open from spring through fall only. Housekeeping Camp is located near the public campgrounds, across from LeConte Lodge, and adjacent to the Merced River.

The camp offers public showers, a store, and a laundromat.

## The Ten Best Views from Above

*I can see for miles and miles.*
— Galen Clark

**Glacier Point:** Not only does the point provide an overwhelming panorama, but it's accessible by car (for better or for worse). The commanding views of Yosemite's high country, Half Dome, Yosemite, Vernal and Nevada Falls, and the valley below are unequaled.

**North Dome:** This promontory allows the best view there is of Half Dome and Tenaya Canyon. Located on the north rim, it can be reached only by foot either from Yosemite Valley (via the Yosemite Falls or Snow Creek trails) or from the Tioga Road via the Porcupine Creek trailhead near Porcupine Flat Campground. All routes are very strenuous. See page 33.

**Eagle Peak:** This lookout is actually the highest rock of the Three Brothers formation. About three miles by trail from the top of Yosemite Falls, the peak offers impressive views of the entire Yosemite region, the Sierra foothills, and the Coast Range far beyond. See page 33.

**Sentinel Dome:** Lacking Glacier Point's glimpses of Yosemite Valley, this dome is almost a thousand feet higher. An unobscured, 360-degree vista presents itself to hikers who make the one-mile walk from the Glacier Point Road. Particularly spectacular under a full moon.

**Tunnel View:** While only part way up the southwestern rim of the valley, this viewpoint just below the Wawona Tunnel on the Wawona Road is a Yosemite classic. More film is used at this location than anywhere else in the park, and for good reason. El Capitan, Bridalveil Fall, and Half Dome couldn't be more photogenic.

**Half Dome:** The only drawback of a perch here is that the view doesn't include Half Dome! Something seems missing from the landscape when you're sitting on this enormous rock that has come to symbolize Yosemite more than any other landmark. The eight-and-a half-mile hike from Happy Isles is quite difficult, though hundreds of people a day undertake it each summer. See page 33.

**Yosemite Point:** About three-quarters of a mile to the east of the top of Yosemite Falls, the point is famous for its proximity to the Lost Arrow Spire, a remarkable freestanding shaft of granite. The view to the south rim is one of the best. See page 33.

**Dewey Point:** The series of viewpoints along the Pohono Trail on the south rim of Yosemite Valley is special. Dewey Point can be reached over the McGurk Meadow trail that heads north from the Glacier Point Road near Bridalveil Creek Campground. Both Dewey and Crocker (a halfmile to the west) Points allow unusual perspectives on El Capitan and Bridalveil Fall.

**Rainbow View:** This location is about a mile and a half up the rockslides trail that crosses the base of El Capitan. While the hike is a rough one over boulders, from the viewpoint roughly opposite the east end of the Wawona Tunnel one is sometimes treated to rainbow displays in Bridalveil Fall during mid-afternoons in summer.

**Taft Point and the Fissures:** Also on the Pohono Trail, these spots are accessed from the same trailhead on the Glacier Point Road that heads to Sentinel Dome. An easy walk leads to Taft Point with its view of the Cathedral Rocks and Spires and the north rim, and to the Fissures which are deep clefts in the rock which drop hundreds of feet towards Yosemite Valley. Check out the echo here.

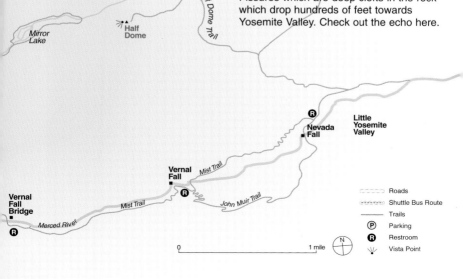

# Wawona, Glacier Point & the Mariposa Grove of Big Trees

Dewey Point

To Glacier Point, Taft Point, Sentinel Dome

Bridalveil Creek

Glacier Point Rd

Mono Meadow

Badger Pass Ski Center (winter only)
Ⓡ

Bridalveil Creek

Chinquapin
Ⓡ

Yosemite West

Wawona Road

Yosemite National Park

Deer Camp

Alder Creek

Chilnualna Creek

Chilnualna Fall

Wawona Dome

Wawona Campground

Chilnualna Falls Rd

Forest Drive

South Fork Merced River

Ⓡ

Wawona Hotel
Ⓟ

Wawona

Pioneer Yosemite History Center

Wawona Meadows & Golf Course

Mariposa Grove
Ⓟ Ⓡ

South Entrance
Ⓡ

## Legend

- Roads
- Trails
- Ⓟ  Parking
- Ⓡ  Restroom
- Vista Point
- Food
- Ranger Station

0          1 mile

N

**41**

To Oakhurst, Fresno

Fish Camp

# South of Yosemite Valley

*T*o the south of Yosemite Valley lies a part of the park that is less busy and noticeably more quiet. Known as the "Wawona District," the south end includes historic Wawona, the world famous Mariposa Grove with its giant sequoias, and the road corridor that leads to Glacier Point. All of these locations are reached primarily by private automobile via the Wawona Road, as only limited, seasonal shuttle and commercial bus service is available.

Mt Clark ▲

Illilouette Creek

Ottoway Lakes

■ Ostrander Ski Hut

*Ostrander Lake*

B U E N A   V I S T A   C R E S T

Buena Vista Peak ▲

*Crescent Lake*   *Johnson Lake*

To Chain Lakes

Buck Camp ■

*South Fork Merced River*

*Star Lakes*

Mt Raymond ▲

Sierra National Forest

Iron ▲ Mountain

## Wawona

*Wawona Meadows themselves might be called the Sleepy Hollow of the West. It is the most peaceful place that I know in America, and comes near being the most idyllic spot I have seen anywhere.*
— Joseph Smeaton Chase

Wawona is a historic community nestled on a beautiful meadow near the South Fork of the Merced River about 25 miles south of Yosemite Valley. The area was settled very early in the park's history and became a stopover point on the stagecoach route to the park. Galen Clark, a significant figure in Yosemite's past (see page 107), built Clark's Station there, and that cabin later grew to become the Wawona Hotel we know today.

To the east of the main road on both sides of the river, a large number of private cabins and homes have been developed. This area, known as Section 35, was held privately for many years before it became part of Yosemite National Park. Known as an "inholding," the tract is still largely privately owned, although the National Park Service has purchased several homes and lots. Many of the residences are available as summer rentals (see the "Lodging" section on page 53).

If you need information, directions, or help, there is an information station in Wawona. To find it, turn off the Wawona Road into the Wawona Hotel grounds. The station is located within the Hill's Studio building that is to the left of the fountain as you face the main hotel section. If there's not parking available, park near the store (just past the gas station) and follow signs up the hill to Hill's Studio. The phone number at the Wawona information station is 375-1416.

### The Wawona Shuttle Bus
During the summer (as funds permit), a free shuttle bus operates in the Wawona area. Generally, the system runs from Memorial Day to Labor Day on a daily basis with stops at the Wawona Campground, the Wawona Store, South Entrance, and the Mariposa Grove of Big Trees. Check the *Yosemite Today* for details, hours, and exact schedules.

### Further Reading
*Map & Guide to Wawona and the Mariposa Grove* by Steven P. Medley. San Francisco, Rufus Graphics, 1997.

**Q:** Name the three U.S. Presidents who have stayed at the Wawona Hotel.

**A:** James Garfield, Ulysses S. Grant, and Rutherford Hayes.

*The Wawona Hotel viewed from the golf course*

## Best Bets South of Yosemite Valley

**The walk to Wawona Point.** Quiet, little-visited, and offering a remarkable view, Wawona Point is the perfect destination for an excursion in the Mariposa Grove. See page 49.

**The outdoor barbecue at the Wawona Hotel.** Enjoy a delicious meal on the lawn under the pine trees at this fine old hotel. Red-checked table cloths in the wilds. See page 44.

**The slopes at Badger Pass.** Every winter, Badger Pass is transformed into a hot bed of skiing and snowboarding activity. Both downhill and cross-country opportunities abound. See page 20.

**Stage coach rides at the Pioneer History Center.** Hold on to your hat on this horse-drawn stage as it makes a short loop to the Wawona Hotel. See page 44.

**The view from Glacier Point.** From the railing at Glacier Point, you are lord (or lady) of all the Yosemite you survey. The view is unforgettable. See page 39.

**A round at the Wawona Golf Course.** Play nine holes at this exceptionally scenic course or just take a walk once it has closed for the day. See page 44.

**Ostrander Ski Hut in winter.** A nine-mile ski from Badger Pass south of the Glacier Point Road, the hut offers shelter and warmth to wilderness skiers. See page 21.

**The Mariposa Grove of Big Trees.** No one comes away unimpressed by these towering sequoias. A world class attraction. See page 48.

## Activities at Wawona

### Step Back in Time

The Pioneer Yosemite History Center is a collection of historic buildings that have been moved from other locations within the park. The center is located near the Wawona Hotel, just east of the gas station (prominent signs will direct you there). During the summer, park rangers and volunteers dress in period costume and populate the buildings. Each building represents a different time period in Yosemite's history, and the rangers engage in "living history," which means that they portray actual Yosemite residents from bygone days. You can try, but you'll have a hard time getting these old-timers to break character.

Interesting attractions are an exhibit of old horse-drawn vehicles, the covered bridge over the South Fork built in the 1870s that has been restored, and a blacksmith who actually practices his craft while you watch.

For a small fee, you can take a short ride on a horse-drawn stage to get a feel for what early trips to Yosemite must have been like. During parts of the year, regular ranger-led tours of the History Center are scheduled (consult the *Yosemite Today* for details).

*The covered bridge, Wawona*

### Hit the Links

A conspicuous adjunct to the Wawona Hotel is its beautifully laid out golf course nearby. Whether you're a golfer or not, a stroll around the 9-hole circuit is both relaxing and replete with scenic vistas. (If you're a non-golfer, take your walk after the course is closed, please!)

The golf course was built in 1917 and features some of the most magnificent golfing holes anywhere. While the lay-out is not particularly long, it features lots of rough and water hazards, and is remarkably challenging. Watch out for deer grazing the fairways, particularly on the first hole.

Golf clubs and carts are available for rent at the Golf Shop, and reserving a tee time is recommended (phone 375-6572).

### Enjoy an Outdoor Barbecue

Every Saturday night during the summer, an old-fashioned barbecue is served outdoors on the expansive lawn of the Wawona Hotel. Red-checked table cloths sport steaks, hamburgers, corn on the cob, western beans, and more. Check at the hotel desk for times and prices.

### Get in the Swim

The South Fork of the Merced River as it runs through Wawona is dotted with swimming holes and beaches. Find a spot to put down your towel and cool off, or try your hand at fishing (see page 29 for general fishing information and regulations). Guests at the Wawona Hotel may use the small swimming pool on the grounds.

### Horse Around a Little

A riding stable is maintained during the summer by DNC Parks & Resorts at Yosemite at the back side of the Pioneer Yosemite History Center on Chilnualna Falls Road (about 1/4 mile off the main highway). Guided horseback rides of varying lengths are offered. Stop by the stable for details or call 375-6502.

### Hike Some More

A variety of hiking awaits you at Wawona, from easy and flat to steep and strenuous. The hiking rules outlined for Yosemite Valley (see page 30) apply in Wawona as well. Give yourself plenty of time and don't undertake more than you're capable of.

### Range with a Ranger

Throughout the year, a program of ranger naturalist activities is presented free of charge to the public in the Wawona area. That program is expanded greatly during the summer. Check the *Yosemite Today* for listings and times.

### Tour an Artist's Studio

The Thomas Hill Studio on the grounds of the Wawona Hotel is usually open in summer as an information station and often features exhibits of the work of Hill along with other art programs. Thomas Hill used the building as a summer studio from 1885 until his death in 1908, and his fine landscape paintings of Yosemite and elsewhere have gained critical acclaim. Check the *Yosemite Today* for hours of operation.

**Q:** What was the toll to use the Mariposa trail through Wawona to Yosemite Valley during the 1850s?

**A:** Man and horse each way, $2.00; pack mule or horse, each way, $2.00; foot man, $1.00.

## Three Hikes from Wawona

**The Meadow Loop**. This pleasant walk begins directly across the Wawona Road from the entry road to the Wawona Hotel. Follow the gravel road about 50 yards across the golf course just into the trees and take the road that leads off to the left. This almost entirely flat route skirts the edge of the Wawona Meadow, then circles back, crosses the Wawona Road, and finishes up behind the Wawona Hotel. Approximately 3 miles total, the loop should take an hour and a half or less. The hike is easy, leisurely, and picturesque.

*The Mariposa Grove Museum*

**Chilnualna Fall.** The trail to this delightful cascade is fairly strenuous, gain-

ing almost 2,500 feet in approximately 4 miles. Start from the trailhead, which is located 1.7 miles east of the main road on Chilnaulna Falls Road. There's parking space on the right for 25 to 30 cars. If the road turns to dirt, you've gone too far. The route is an enjoyable one through manzanita, deer brush, and bear clover, and finally meets with Chilnualna Creek. The fall, instead of leaping and free-falling from some precipice, drops through a narrow chasm in a furious rush. Allow 6 to 8 hours for this 8-mile round trip. Carry lots of water in the summer when temperatures can be extreme.

**Mariposa Big Trees.** Starting behind the Wawona Hotel is a long, uphill climb to the Mariposa Grove of giant sequoias. Passing through forest most of the way, the trail offers excellent views of the Wawona Basin and Wawona Dome as it nears the big trees. The trail ends at the Mariposa Grove Museum in the Upper Grove near the fallen Tunnel Tree. Because the elevation gain is 3,000 feet in 6.5 miles, this hike is for the well-conditioned only. For an easier alternative, take the summer shuttle bus to the Mariposa Grove and hike back to Wawona. Figure on spending 8 to 10 hours making the up-and-back trip of 13 miles.

## Activities Along the Glacier Point Road

The road to Glacier Point leaves the Wawona Road at Chinquapin junction, 9 miles south of Yosemite Valley and 12 miles north of Wawona. The route winds 16 miles to the amazing promontory at Glacier Point, passing a variety of sites and attractions along the way, most of them short hikes from the road.

The route is open to the point during the three milder seasons, but in winter the road is plowed of snow only as far as Badger Pass, the downhill ski area 6 miles from Chinquapin. Be sure to carry tire chains in your car if you're heading out the Glacier Point Road during the "off-season."

### Stare at the Stars
During the summer, ranger naturalists maintain a large telescope at Glacier Point and schedule regular evening programs that make use of it. There aren't many better spots for gazing at the heavens, plus you'll have the help of knowledgeable astronomers. Check the *Yosemite Today* for dates and times and for the schedule of other ranger-led programs and hikes at Glacier Point and Bridalveil Creek Campground.

### Hike, Hike, and More Hike
Given its proximity to the south rim of Yosemite Valley, the Glacier Point Road provides a series of natural trailheads for spectacular day hikes. And thanks to DNC, you have the option of walking all the way down to Yosemite Valley without needing to retrieve your car. During the summer, a "Hiker's Bus" is operated from the valley to spots along the road all the way to Glacier Point. Call 372-1240 for information.

### Strap on Some Skis or a Board
Badger Pass, six miles from Chinquapin out the Glacier Point Road, is the center of Yosemite ski activity during the winter. Not only are there ski lifts, ski and snowboard rentals, and a lodge, but cross-country skiers are encouraged to utilize the groomed tracks out the Glacier Point Road (see page 20).

**Q:** Which landmark near the Glacier Point Road offers a 360 degree view of the park and is the location of a much-photographed Jeffrey pine?

**A:** Sentinel Dome (the Jeffrey pine died several years ago).

## Five Great Hikes from the Glacier Point Road

**Dewey Point.** One of the most interesting perspectives on Bridalveil Fall and El Capitan is afforded by this commanding viewpoint (7,385 feet). The trail starts two-tenths of a mile west of (before you get to) Bridalveil Creek Campground on the Glacier Point Road. While there are trail markers on both sides of the road, you will want to head north. The route meanders through forest and meadows, intersects with the Pohono Trail (go left), then extends to the valley rim. While there's not much elevation gain or loss, the round trip is approximately 7 miles. Allow 4 to 6 hours for the out-and-back hike.

**Mono Meadow and Mt. Starr King View.** From the parking area 2.5 miles beyond Bridalveil Creek Campground on the Glacier Point Road, this trail leads to the east and to a terrific spot for admiring Mt. Starr King, Half Dome, and Clouds Rest. You will drop steeply for a half-mile to Mono Meadow, then continue a mile further to an unmarked clearing where the view is an obvious one. Stop short of the switchbacks down to Illilouette Creek. The three mile round trip (a little strenuous on the way back) should take about 3 hours.

**Taft Point.** Unusual rock formations and an overhanging lookout point reward hikers on this short route. Start at the parking lot on the Glacier Point Road about six miles past Bridalveil Creek Campground (it's on the left, when you first catch a glimpse of Sentinel Dome). The trail is mostly flat and slightly downhill to the Fissures (wide gaps in the rock hundreds of feet deep) and Taft Point, where you'll be standing on the only solid object between you and the valley floor leagues below you. Be thorough in your investigation of the point, which offers up several unique views. It's just over two miles round-trip; give yourself two hours.

**Sentinel Dome.** The trailheads for this hike and the one to Taft Point are the same. Park on the left about six miles past Bridalveil Creek Campground on the Glacier Point Road (it's about at the spot where you first eye Sentinel Dome). The 1.1 mile hike to the top is a small price to pay for the 360 degree panorama of Yosemite's unbelievable landscape. You'll be at 8,122 feet (more than 4,000 feet above the Yosemite Valley floor); it's a good idea to have a park map for landmark identification. Try this easy hike at sunrise or sunset or on the night of a full moon. The round trip requires about two hours.

*View from Glacier Point*

**Yosemite Valley.** Take the "Hiker's Bus" (see page 46) or have someone shuttle you to Glacier Point and walk back down to Yosemite Valley over the Four-Mile Trail (4.8 miles) or via the Panorama Cliffs Trail by way of Nevada and Vernal Falls (8.5 miles). The Four-Mile Trail begins to the left of Glacier Point and follows a series of switchbacks down the face of the south valley wall. It terminates about a mile west of Yosemite Village on Southside Drive. The Panorama Trail begins to the right of the point, heading south to the top of Illilouette Fall, then back north and east to Nevada Fall (see page 333). There are two routes to the valley (either the "horse trail" or the Mist Trail, see page 33) and trail's end at Happy Isles (shuttle bus stop # 16). Figure on 3 to 4 hours to hike the Four-MileTrail and allow 6 to 8 hours to travel the Panorama Cliffs route.

Half
Dome ▲

Vernal
Fall ■

_orama Cliffs Trail_

Mount
Starr
King
▲

_Illilouette Creek_

## Activities at the Mariposa Grove of Big Trees

Located at the southernmost end of Yosemite, the Mariposa Grove is the largest stand of giant sequoias *(sequoiadendron giganteum)* in the park. These ancient monarchs are inadequately described with numbers, but how else do you do it? Some of the trees are 2,000 years old, others reach almost 300 feet into the sky, still others are more than 50 feet around. A typical mature sequoia weighs in at over 2 million pounds.

Notable trees here are the Grizzly Giant, almost three millennia old and 96 feet around at its base, the fallen Wawona Tunnel Tree, through which a hole was cut that allowed thousands of automobiles and other vehicles to pass through and be photographed before the tree toppled in 1969, and many others. There are over 500 sequoias here in two related groves, the Upper and Lower.

You may drive to the edge of the Lower Grove, where hiking trails lead out among the trees. The road to the Mariposa Grove is oftentimes closed in winter when the snow is deep.

### Ride the Open-Air Tram

If you'd rather not hike into the Mariposa Grove, buy a ticket and board one of the open-air trams that will carry you out among these magnificent giants. In summer 2004, the fee was $11 for adults and $5.50 for children 4-12 (children under 4 ride free, and there is a discount for seniors 62 or over). The trams cover a 5-mile loop and leave about every 20 minutes.

The first tram departs at 9 a.m., and the last tram leaves at 4 p.m. The trip takes slightly less than an hour, but you'd be well-advised to get off the tram and spend a little time walking in the grove. The trams do not operate during the winter.

There are three regular stopping points along the route: the Grizzly Giant, the fallen Tunnel Tree, and the Mariposa Grove Museum. On your way back down, consider getting off at the Grizzly Giant and walking the eight-tenths of a mile back to the parking lot. It's all downhill and remarkably relaxing.

Be sure to visit the Mariposa Grove Museum where there are exhibits about

the giant sequoias and books and other literature for sale. Restrooms are located there, too.

*Mariposa Grove of Big Trees*

### Walk in the Sequoia Forest

All trails into the Mariposa Grove of Big Trees are uphill. From the trailhead at the far end of the parking lot, there is an elevation gain of about 1,000 feet to the Upper Grove where the fallen Wawona Tunnel Tree is located, a distance of 2.5 miles. The going is gradual, however (22 children from Mrs. McDaniel's second grade class made it up and back!), and walking is the best way to appreciate the majesty and serenity of these stately trees. Be sure to check park hiking regulations before you take off (see page 30).

### Notable Sequoias of the Mariposa Grove

| Name | Diameter at Base | Height |
|---|---|---|
| Grizzly Giant | 31 ft | 209 ft. |
| California Tree | 23 ft. | 232 ft. |
| Faithful Couple | 40 ft. | 248 ft. |
| Columbia Tree | 28 ft. | 290 ft. |
| Clothespin Tree | 22 ft. | 266 ft. |
| General Grant Tree | 29 ft. | 290 ft. |
| Washington Tree | 30 ft. | 238 ft. |
| Lafayette Tree | 31 ft. | 267 ft. |

## Three Easier Hikes in the Mariposa Grove

**The Grizzly Giant.** From the parking lot it's only eight-tenths of a mile and a 400-foot climb to the Grizzly Giant, one of the largest trees in the Mariposa Grove. Along the way you'll encounter lots of other sequoias and get a personal perspective on the mammoth scale of these trees. Allow from 1 to 2 hours for the round trip.

**Wawona Point.** This excellent lookout on the entire Wawona basin is a short walk from the top of the Mariposa Grove. Get off the tram at the fallen Wawona Tunnel Tree and walk back to the north to the Galen Clark Tree, where the old road to Wawona Point branches off. Ask your tram driver for directions if you need them. The walk is only one-half mile, and you'll be able to see back to the Wawona Meadow and golf course, with views to the east of Wawona Dome. The round trip walk should take you less than an hour.

**Mariposa Grove Parking Lot from the Wawona Tunnel Tree.** It's always easier to hike downhill, so why not ride the tram to the top of the grove and get off at the Wawona Tunnel Tree? The hike down through the Upper and Lower Groves leads past the Mariposa Grove Museum and just about every significant sequoia in the area. It's only two and a half miles back to your car, and shouldn't require more than two to three hours to complete.

**Q:** When did the Wawona Tunnel Tree fall over and why?

**A:** In 1969 as a result of the tunnel cut through its base, enormous impact to its root system from cars and people, and a heavy snow load.

Mariposa Grove

## Wawona History

The Wawona area was first settled by Yosemite pioneer Galen Clark (see page 107), who homesteaded 160 acres there in 1856. Though probably not deliberately, Clark selected a spot that was almost exactly half-way between Mariposa and Yosemite on the route that developed for visitors. Clark seized the opportunity and built a rustic lodging house for travelers that was known as "Clark's Station."

Though Galen Clark recognized the potential of his way station, he proved unable to fulfill it. His management of Clark's Station was poor, and he invested considerable funds in completing the Mariposa stage road to Wawona. Financial pressure forced Clark to take on Edwin Moore as a full partner in 1869, and all signs indicated that Clark's fortunes had turned.

But over the next five years, ill-advised investments in mining ventures and land purchases along with the completion of the Coulterville and Big Oak Flat Roads into Yosemite Valley spelled doom for Clark and Moore. They were forced to sell their lodging house and related properties to the Washburn Brothers in December of 1874.

*U.S. Cavalry at Camp A. E. Wood*

The Washburns were an enterprising group of three brothers, who came to California from Putney, Vermont. They undertook a number of ventures in the Mariposa area before purchasing Clark and Moore's. It was their New England background that led them to cover the existing bridge over the South Fork of the Merced; it's the same bridge that leads into the Pioneer Yosemite History Center today.

Contemporaneously with their acquisition of the Wawona traveler's stop, the Washburns began work on the completion of the stage road from Wawona to Yosemite Valley. In this way they hoped to compete with the other routes. They finished the job in June of 1875, and their plan began to meet with success.

In 1876 the Washburns put up the long white structure that stands just to the right of the main hotel building today. And when that building burnt in 1878, the two-story structure that is still used as the main hotel building went up the next year. Until 1882

the inn was known as Big Tree Station when it officially became the Wawona Hotel. Additional buildings went up over the years.

Congress established Yosemite National Park in 1890 and directed that the U.S. Army should be responsible for managing it. Because Yosemite Valley and the Mariposa Grove of Big Trees had already been granted to the State of California and were not part of the national park, locating park headquarters became a challenge. As Wawona was one of the few developed areas within the new park (though not part of it) and for other reasons, it was selected as the summer command for Army personnel.

Known as Camp A. E. Wood, headquarters were located on the site of the present Wawona Campground. For sixteen summers cavalry troops from the San Francisco area occupied the camp and engaged in caring for the new park. Among their many activities were exploring and mapping, trail building, fish planting, and enforcing anti-hunting and trespassing regulations. When the state grant and Yosemite National Park were combined in 1906, Camp A. E. Wood was abandoned and Army headquarters were relocated to Yosemite Valley.

Over the years, changes to Wawona generally came with changes in transportation. Following the completion of the Wawona Stage Road, the Washburn's stage company flourished and visitation grew. In 1914, automobiles first navigated the road between Wawona and Yosemite Valley. The Wawona Hotel management recognized that the automobile travelers preferred more recreational opportunities, and proceeded to build a dance floor, soda fountain, croquet court, swimming tank, and golf course over the next fifteen years.

As the Wawona Hotel prospered, so did the community in Section 35 (the number assigned to the plot of land in its legal description) that included several homesteads and housed workers for the hotel and for other support services. When most of the Wawona region was added to Yosemite National Park in 1932, only Section 35 remained in private ownership. It is this area of Wawona where many private homes, cabins, and visitor rentals are located today (see page 42).

### Further Reading

*Yosemite's Historic Wawona* by Shirley Sargent. Yosemite: Flying Spur Press, 1979.

*Galen Clark: Yosemite Guardian* by Shirley Sargent. Yosemite: Flying Spur Press, 1981.

## Camping South of Yosemite Valley

*T*he campgrounds in this part of the park tend to be less busy and crowded, though in summer they are full practically every night. Advance reservations are required for the Wawona Campground between May and September, but Bridalveil Creek Campground is operated on a first-come, first-served basis when it is open between July and September. In campgrounds where no reservations are allowed, visitors will benefit by arriving as early as possible to arrange for a camping spot, because check out time is 12 noon.

Camping regulations are roughly the same as those for Yosemite Valley (see page 34). Pets are allowed in designated sites in both the Wawona and Bridalveil Creek Campgrounds, and there are no showers in any park campground. The camping limit is 14 days in summer south of Yosemite Valley, and a 30-day limit applies the rest of the year. A total of 30 camping days per calendar year is permitted in the park.

**Wawona Campground:** This popular spot is located at the 4,000-foot elevation on the banks of the South Fork of the Merced River approximately 25 miles south of Yosemite Valley on the Wawona Road. The daily fee for the 93 sites here is $18, and the campground is open all year (prepare for extreme cold and snow in the winter, however).

**Bridalveil Creek Campground:** You'll find this group of 110 campsites nine miles out the Glacier Point Road from Chinquapin (about 25 miles from Yosemite Valley). Open from June or July through September, the campground is much cooler than Yosemite Valley or Wawona given its location at over 7,000 feet. The nightly fee is $12.

**Group Campgrounds:** Sections of the Wawona and Bridalveil Creek Campgrounds have been set aside for use by organized groups only. Reservations can be made through NPRS (see page 12); groups of between 13 and 30 people are allowed in each campsite, where only tent camping is allowed. Pets are not permitted in group sites. There are also horse camps at both the Wawona and Bridalveil Creek Campgrounds. For more information, call (209) 375-9520.

**Q:** How fast can a backpacker carrying a pack that's one-fifth his or her body weight expect to travel?

**A:** About two horizontal miles per hour. Add one hour for each 1,000 feet of elevation gain.

*South Fork of the Merced River, Wawona*

## Gas, Food & Lodging South of Yosemite Valley

### Gas

The only gas station in this part of the park is located in Wawona, just north of the Wawona Hotel on the main highway. The self-serve facility accepts major credit cards (it's a Chevron station), it's open year-round, and tire chains are available.

For towing services, call 372-8320 at any time of the day or night.

### Food: Restaurants

For other than snacks and simple sandwiches, there's only one choice in the south end of the park—the Wawona Hotel Dining Room. If you're near the South Entrance, there are a number of good restaurants along Highway 41 between Fish Camp and Oakhurst, all within a half hour's drive. The following places to eat are open seasonally only; be sure to check the *Yosemite Today* for dates and hours of operation.

### Wawona Hotel Dining Room:

Serving breakfast, lunch, and dinner from Easter week through October and on weekends and holidays in the fall and winter. Located in the Victorian main building at the hotel, the dining room has retained a historic feel. The sepiatone photographs by Carleton Watkins and the sequoia cone light fixtures are perfect touches in this charming, multi-windowed facility. The food is fine, the wine list good, and there's a full bar. In summer, there are a few tables on the porch for outdoor dining, and they also serve in the bar area. There's cocktail service on the verandas and in the lobby lounge. Lunch and Sunday brunch are served buffet style. On Saturdays in summer try the outdoor barbeque on the hotel lawn. Reservations are advised for groups of ten or more; call 375-1425 for more information. Moderate to expensive.

### Wawona Golf Shop Snack Stand:

Open spring through fall inside the golf shop at the Wawona Hotel. Cold drinks, hot dogs, pre-packaged sandwiches, and other simple items are available if you're in a hurry or need a light meal or snack. Moderate prices.

### Glacier Point Snack Stand: A summer and fall operation (10 a.m. to 5 p.m.) with a limited menu. Primarily providing munchies for visitors to Glacier Point. Moderate prices.

### Food: Groceries

Campers, vacation home renters, and park visitors have the following two choices for groceries in the park south of Yosemite Valley. Check the *Yosemite Today* for operating hours, or call the indicated numbers.

### Wawona Grocery Store: Located adjacent to the gas station just off the main highway and north of the Wawona Hotel. Phone 375-6574.

### The Pine Tree Market: You'll find this store in the heart of the community of North Wawona. It's less than a mile east of the main highway on Chilnualna Falls Road. Phone 375-6343.

Inexpensive: dinner for one adult might cost up to $10. Moderate: dinner for one adult might cost from $10 to $20. Expensive: dinner for one adult might cost over $20.

*Wawona Hotel*

# Lodging

Wawona is the only area in the park where the majority of the lodging facilities is not operated by DNC, the park's main concessioner. The Wawona Hotel is part of the DNC system, and to reserve a room there, you should follow the steps which are detailed on page 11. You must contact each of the other lodging providers directly to reserve from them.

The quoted rates for the following listed lodging facilities are approximate only, based on double occupancy, vary with the seasons, and are subject to change.

*Wawona Dome*

## Wawona Hotel

Open from Easter week through October and on weekends and holidays through Christmas. This is the oldest resort hotel in California; the structure to the right of the main hotel building was built in 1879. The whitewashing, wide porches, well-kept grounds, and an old-fashioned bathing tank (we call them swimming pools now) all suggest another era in Yosemite's history. It's a remarkably peaceful and relaxing setting, but guests should keep in mind that some of the rooms are 100 years old. Rooms with bath rent for $166 in season ($149 in the off season), while rooms that utilize a community bath-room are priced at $113 in season ($92 in the off season). Rates are scheduled to increase in March, 2002.

Besides a dining room (described at left), the Wawona Hotel incorporates a golf course with pro shop and snack bar, tennis courts, and a cocktail lounge.

## The Redwoods Guest Cottages

Open year around. This is a collection of about 130 privately-owned vacation homes and cabins available for rental on a daily or weekly basis. Located in the privately-held section of Wawona near the South Fork of the Merced (approximately 1 mile out Chilnualna Falls Road), the rentals vary in size from 1 to 6 bedrooms. Rates vary with the seasons and range from $143 to $643 plus tax per night for units that all have kitchens and fireplaces; there is a two-night minimum. For information call 375-6666, or write to PO Box 2085, Wawona, CA 95389. The web site address is www.redwoodsguestcottages.com.

## Yosemite West Condominiums

Open year around. Just beyond the park boundary, but accessible only via park roads, these rental units are situated about half-way between Yosemite Valley and Wawona. Their proximity (8 miles) to the Badger Pass ski area has made the condos a favorite of winter visitors. But cool summer temperatures and the short drive to Yosemite Valley (about half an hour) make Yosemite West popular other parts of the year, as well. Rates start from $99 to $129 (peak season), depending on unit size. Information can be had by calling 1-888-296-7364, a toll-free number. The web site address is www.yosemitewest.com.

## Yosemite West Lodging

Open all year. This company handles the rental of a collection of studios, apartments, townhouses, duplexes, individual cottages, vacation homes, and mountain homes, all in the Yosemite West development. These are located just west of the park less than one mile south of Chinquapin off the Wawona Road (only 15 miles from Yosemite Valley and 8 miles from Badger Pass). All units have televisions and kitchens. Rates range all the way from $85 to $345 per night, and discounts are available for longer stays. For reservations, etc., call (559) 642-2211, or write PO Box 36, Yosemite National Park, CA 95389. The web site address is also www.yosemitewest.com.

**Q:** What was the source of ice for the Wawona Hotel each winter from 1886 until 1934?

**A:** Ice was cut by hand at Stella Lake, which was created by damming and diverting the South Fork of the Merced River about a quarter mile upstream from the hotel. The lake froze to a depth of about six inches.

**Q:** What was the first public lodging house developed in the Wawona area?

**A:** Clark's Station, built by Galen Clark in 1856.

# Hetch Hetchy, The Tioga Road & Tuloumne Meadows

Lake Vernon

Laurel Lake

Lake Eleanor

Wapama Falls

Tueeulala Falls

Hetch Hetchy Reservoir

Tuolumne River

O'Shaughnessy Dam

Hetch Hetchy Backpackers Campground
(Wilderness Permit - Required)

Hetch Hetchy Entrance

Harden Lake

To San Francisco

Evergreen Road

Hetch Hetchy Road

Bald Mountain

White Wolf

Lukens Lake

Tioga Road

To San Francisco

Big Oak Flat Entrance

South Fork Tuolumne River

Yosemite Creek

120

Hodgdon Meadow

Tuolumne Grove

road closed late fall - late spring

Merced Grove

Crane Flat

Tamarack Flat

Yosemite Valley

Yosemite Falls

Big Oak Flat Road

El Capitan

Bridalveil Fall

Sentinel Dome

El Portal

El Portal Rd

Arch Rock Entrance

Glacier Point Rd

To Merced

Merced River

140

Wawona Road

To Fresno

Roads

Trails

(P) Parking

(R) Restroom

Vista Point

Food

N

0                    5 miles

# North of Yosemite Valley

Over two-thirds of Yosemite National Park lie north of Yosemite Valley, much of that region being wilderness. The area is made accessible primarily by the Tioga Road, the only trans-Sierra crossing between Walker Pass in Kern County and Sonora Pass to the north. Spectacular high country terrain, brilliant blue lakes, and astounding granite peaks are reached via this route that leads through Tuolumne Meadows, the largest subalpine meadows in the Sierra Nevada. The road crests the range at 9,945-foot Tioga Pass.

Spiller Lake

Soldier Lake

McCabe Lakes

Roosevelt Lake

Mt Conness ▲

Young Lakes

Glen Aulin High ⛺ Sierra Camp

## Tuolumne Meadows

Dog Lake

To Tioga Pass Entrance/ Lee Vining

Lembert ▲ Dome

Lyell Fork

Grant Lakes

Facilities along Tioga Road available summer only

Tioga Road

Tuolumne Meadows Visitor Center

Tuolumne Meadows Campground

Mt Hoffmann ▲

May Lake

Cathedral Peak ▲

Elizabeth Lake

Tenaya Lake

Evelyn Lake

Porcupine △ Flat

120

Olmsted ↑ Point

Vogelsang △ High Sierra Camp

Sunrise △ High Sierra Camp

North Dome

Bernice Lake

Valley Visitor Center

Tenaya Creek

Clouds Rest ▲

Half Dome ▲

Vernal Fall

Nevada Fall

Merced River

Merced Lake

Washburn Lake

Glacier Point ▲

Illilouette Creek

Mt Clark ▲

Ostrander Lake

Ottoway Lakes

Edna Lake

## Best Bets North of Yosemite Valley

*Mt. Hoffmann*

**The summit of Mount Hoffmann.** This is the geographic center of Yosemite, with extraordinary views in every direction. See page 61.

**The beach at Tenaya Lake.** Unbelievably fine on a warm day, a terrific spot anytime. Enjoy a picnic, swim, or simply take a nap. See page 61.

**The turnout at Olmsted Point.** To see the vast expanse of glacier-carved granite is worth the stop alone. But there's much more, and marmots, too. See page 61.

**The hike to the Merced Grove.** Flat, easy, and quiet. Plus this is Yosemite's most remote and least-visited sequoia grove. See page 58.

**A meal on the porch of White Wolf Lodge.** Lunch and dinner are likely times to sit outside at this quaint spot and watch the White Wolf meadow do whatever meadows do. See page 70.

**A visit to Hetch Hetchy Reservoir.** This body of water occupies a valley which has been characterized as Yosemite Valley's little brother. It has retained much of its beauty, and offers great hiking. See page 57.

**The trail into Lyell Canyon.** The Lyell Fork of the Tuolumne River is one of the park's most peaceful and inspiring settings. The trail leads to and along its course. See page 67.

**The High Sierra Camps.** Whether you hike the full loop or visit just one of these five backcountry encampments, the experience will be unique. Stop for a mindblowing meal, or pamper yourself by staying over. See page 64.

*Tenaya Lake*

*White Wolf Lodge*

## Hetch Hetchy

*Whatever Hetch Hetchy means—grass, seeds, trees—it is no longer relevant; everything is covered by water.*
—Peter Browning

The Hetch Hetchy area of Yosemite, as it is called in this book, includes the portion of the park that is found on its western boundary along the Big Oak Flat Road north of Crane Flat, and along the Evergreen and Hetch Hetchy Roads (see map). The region is best known for its two groves of giant sequoias (the Merced and Tuolumne Groves), and for the Hetch Hetchy Reservoir on the Tuolumne River.

National Park Service headquarters here are located at the Big Oak Flat Entrance where there is a ranger station (phone 379-1899), a NPRS reservation office, a small visitor center and book sales area, a wilderness permit and reservation office, and public restrooms. If you've entered the park from the west over Highway 120, this is a good place to orient yourself; Yosemite Valley is still a 25-mile drive. There's also an entrance station at Mather, about eight miles from the Big Oak Flat Entrance on the way to Hetch Hetchy.

The route to Hetch Hetchy Reservoir is over Evergreen Road, located just north of the park off Highway 120. If traveling from the south, leave the park through the Big Oak Flat Entrance. The right turn onto Evergreen Road is one mile past the entrance station. From the north, turn left on Evergreen Road one mile before you reach the park on Highway 120. Hetch Hetchy is 16 miles out this road which becomes Hetch Hetchy Road at Camp Mather (bear right at the intersection).

### Hetch Hetchy: The Dam

Many wonder how a facility like Hetch Hetchy Reservoir came to be sited within the boundaries of a national park. It wasn't easy or quick, but when the political struggle ended, the scenic qualities of Hetch Hetchy Valley had been "submerged" for the good of the citizens of San Francisco and their thirsts.

The city had been looking for a dependable mountain water supply, when shortly after the turn of the century, Hetch Hetchy was proposed as the perfect location for a dam site. The notion of a reservoir in Yosemite was not universally attractive, however, and John Muir, the Sierra Club, and others opposed the project and fought it for many years. On several occasions the Hetch Hetchy project was outright rejected. But the city fathers were persistent, and in 1913, the Raker Bill granting San Francisco permission to dam the Tuolumne River at Hetch Hetchy was passed in Congress.

The loss of the fight to save Hetch Hetchy was devastating for Muir. Many believe that his efforts severely drained him, left him exhausted, and contributed greatly to his death about a year later. On the other hand, the reservoir proved an enormous success for the City of San Francisco, which still relies on the project for the bulk of its water and power.

The dam was constructed beginning in 1919 and took about four years to finish. The resulting reservoir is 8 miles long, has a capacity of 117,400,000 gallons, and covers 1,861 surface acres (3 square miles). The dam itself is 410 feet high, 910 feet long, and 308 feet thick at its base that tapers to 24 feet at the top. One interesting fact about the Hetch Hetchy project is that the water in system pipelines flows all the way to San Francisco by gravity!

## Activities in the Hetch Hetchy Area

The Hetch Hetchy area is best enjoyed in spring and fall, though it's remarkably mild some winters. The habitat of this region is more foothill than montane, and there are lots of gray pines, manzanita, and lower-elevation wildflowers. Stop at the Big Oak Flat Visitor Center (at the park entrance) to get oriented.

*Merced Grove*

### Walk Through the Merced Grove

Yosemite's quietest stand of sequoias is the Merced Grove, accessible only on foot. It's a two-mile hike into the grove from the trailhead on the Big Oak Flat Road. Located 3.5 miles north of Crane Flat or 4.5 miles south of the Big Oak Flat Entrance, the trailhead is marked by a post labeled B-10 and a road sign.

Follow the dirt road for about a mile, then take the left fork down into the grove. This is the park's smallest group of sequoias (about twenty trees), which was probably first discovered in 1833 by the Joseph Reddeford Walker party. Look for the old Merced Grove cabin that was built as a ranger/entrance station, but is no longer used for that purpose.

These sequoias convey the silent majesty that has characterized them for thousands of years. The absence of motorized vehicles and the solitude are a real treat for hikers to the Merced Grove. Allow 3 hours for the 4-mile round trip.

### Hike the Tuolumne Grove

The former route of the Big Oak Flat Road leads downhill from Crane Flat into the Tuolumne Grove of Big Trees, a cluster of about forty-five sequoias. Open to traffic until 1993, this dirt road drops steeply for about a mile where the first big trees can be spotted. An interesting attraction in the grove is the "Dead Giant" tree, a lifeless but still-standing partial tree that has been driven through by thousands of wagons and automobiles since it was tunneled out in 1878 (but no longer). There's also a self-guiding nature trail in the grove, a half-mile in length, that should take about 30 minutes to walk.

The trail to the Tuolumne Grove takes off near Crane Flat. From the intersection of the Big Oak Flat Road and the Tioga Road, take the Tioga Road one mile to the east (towards Tuolumne Meadows). Turn left at road marker O-1 and park in the lot there. The route is obvious; the round trip of about two miles is relatively easy, though it's all uphill on the way back.

### Let Them Entertain You

In summer, National Park Service rangers conduct a variety of walks, programs, and campfires. Activities are centered at Crane Flat Campground and in the Tuolumne Grove, though other locales are used from time to time. Check the *Yosemite Today* under White Wolf/Crane Flat/Big Oak Flat Visitor Activities for specific details and times.

### Lookout for Fire

The Crane Flat Fire Lookout is staffed during the summer when the National Park Service watches the surrounding forests for signs of smoke. Visitors are welcome at the facility that can be reached over a primitive road leading off to the east less than one mile north of Crane Flat on the Big Oak Flat Road. The uphill trip to the lookout is one and a half miles.

Be sure to watch for fire and other emergency vehicles along the way. The view from the lookout is a special one with glimpses of the park in every direction. It's also fun to ski here in winter.

**Q:** Who was the first Euro-American to visit Hetch Hetchy Valley?

**A:** Joseph Screech in 1850.

**Q:** When and where were the Big Trees discovered by Euro-Americans?

**A:** It is probable that the Joseph Reddeford Walker party discovered the giant sequoias in either the Tuolumne or Merced Grove in 1833.

*Hikers at Hetch Hetchy*

## Hike Hetch Hetchy

T hough the once beautiful valley of Hetch Hetchy might be lost forever, many of its scenic wonders can still be appreciated. Tueeulala and Wapama Falls still thunder from the north rim, Kolana Rock still rises imposingly from the reservoir's southern shore, and a remarkable variety of plant and animal life still populates the perimeter of the place.

While Hetch Hetchy is at roughly the same elevation as Yosemite Valley, it's a much warmer spot. In the middle of summer it's downright hot. Perfect months for day hiking here are October through May. You'd be amazed at how warm the north side of the reservoir can be in the dead of winter.

The main trail at Hetch Hetchy leads over the top of the dam, through a tunnel, and along the north edge. The undulating route passes Tueeulala Falls, Wapama Falls (about two miles from the dam), and eventually Rancheria Falls (six and a half miles out). Hike as far or as little as you like. In spring, be prepared at Wapama Falls for high water and heavy mist that sometimes force closure of the trail. Retrace your steps back to the dam.

Fishing is allowed in Hetch Hetchy Reservoir, but swimming and boating are not.

## The Tioga Road

Originally a wagon road across Tioga Pass built by the Great Consolidated Silver Company in 1883, the Tioga Road literally splits Yosemite National Park in two. Improved to its present condition and alignment in 1961, the road opened up some of Yosemite's most stunning country and allowed access to previously remote high country destinations. Today the Tioga Road corridor is rife with scenic and recreational opportunities.

For the purposes of this book, the Tioga Road refers to the area of the park along the Tioga Road (which extends from Crane Flat to Tioga Pass some 46 miles east) except for the Tuolumne Meadows area.

*Lembert Dome*

Visitors should be aware that the Tioga Road is not open all year. Heavy snows require the National Park Service to close the road (from November until May or June, usually), though snow is a possibility in any season; be sure to carry tire chains when driving this route in spring or fall. Typically mild summer weather attracts both recreationists and travelers headed east in large numbers.

There are plenty of options for fun along the road, with multiple campgrounds, trailheads, lakes, streams, and scenic views to choose from. If you need information or assistance, there is a ranger station at Tioga Pass Entrance (as well as the Tuolumne Meadows Ranger Station described on page 65.)

*Tioga Pass Entrance*

### The "Controversial" Tioga Road

In the 1950s, when the National Park Service made the decision to re-align and complete the "modern" Tioga Road, discussions ensued over whether the 21-mile central portion of the new road should be routed via the "high" or "scenic" line or along the general route of the old Tioga Road. Studies involving discussions with various cooperating groups, the Secretary of the Interior, and other interested parties became fraught with controversy.

Objections arose specifically from certain conservationists and the Bureau of Public Roads after it had been decided to proceed on the "high" route selected and approved years earlier. Changes to meet improved safety standards met resistance from such people as David Brower, executive secretary of the Sierra Club, and nature photographer Ansel Adams.

The Bureau of Public Roads believed that a wider road with wider shoulders was necessary so that cars could pull off the road in emergencies. The Park Service, meanwhile, wanted a safe width of road with narrow shoulders and with turnouts only where the terrain permitted to avoid scars from cuts and fills as much as possible plus higher costs.

The matter was finally settled in favor of the two-foot shoulders with few turnouts except for one section where the shoulder had to be widened to provide the necessary stability. Conservationists, however, continued to object to the blasting and gouging methods used and the resulting scars on the face of the glacially-polished granite surfaces at Olmsted Point.

Actual construction of the new central section began in 1957, and it officially opened in June 1961. Sections of the old Tioga Road were retained, such as that leaving the new road just east of the White Wolf intersection and winding down to the Yosemite Creek Campground; another short section climbs over Snow Flat to the May Lake Trail junction. Shorter sections still serve campgrounds along the old road.

from *Yosemite Historic Resource Study, Vol. 2,* by Linda Wedel Green.

## Activities Along the Tioga Road

Whether you're just passing through or making a leisurely trip along the Tioga Road, your experience will be a better one if you know where you are and what you're seeing. A valuable aid in this regard is *The Yosemite Road Guide*, an informative book keyed to markers along the way. It's available at stores throughout the park or from the Yosemite Association. How else will you know about "Smoky Jack," the old Tioga Road, Siesta Lake, and the ghost forest?

### Get in Over Your Head
The best place to have a swim along the Tioga Road is Tenaya Lake. The park's largest lake, it is located approximately 8 miles west of Tuolumne Meadows, or 30 miles east of Crane Flat. The inviting sandy beach on the eastern shore is a good bet, but be prepared for some cold water. Tenaya Lake is also a favorite of sailboarders, windsurfers, and sailboaters (check with a ranger for regulations). Use the dressing and bathrooms in the parking lot just east of the lake. If it's too cold to swim, have a picnic in this dramatic setting.

### Be Programmed
During summer, ranger-naturalists offer free programs for visitors at various locations along theTioga Road. Likely meeting places are White Wolf and Tenaya Lake, but check the *Yosemite Today* for details.

### Hike All You Like
The territory stretching out to the north and south of the Tioga Road is a veritable hiker's wonderland. From numerous points along the route trails lead into a landscape unequalled anywhere in the world. Hikes range from easy to very strenuous, and become more difficult with the increased elevation. Follow basic hiking precautions (see page 30), and in this high country setting, stay hydrated by drinking lots of liquids. The most common hiking-related ailment is altitude sickness; consider spending a day or so getting acclimatized before starting to hike.

For those hikers who travel to Yosemite without a car or who wish to leave their vehicle in Yosemite Valley, there's a hiker's bus operated by the DNC, traversing the length of the Tioga Road each day from July 1 to Labor Day. You can arrange to get off at trailheads along the way. The bus returns to Yosemite Valley every afternoon. For information, call 372-1240.

### Wet A Line
Fishing can be amazingly good along the Tioga Road. Spots like Lukens Lake, Harden Lake, Tenaya Lake, and May Lake (all described in this chapter) are home to many feisty, if somewhat small, trout. Yosemite Creek and the Dana Fork of the Tuolumne River can also yield up a fish or two. The general park fishing regulations apply (see page 29); check with a park ranger for any special rules.

### Check Out Half Dome's Back Side
One of Yosemite's most remarkable scenic overlooks is found at Olmsted Point, and it shouldn't be missed. This major pullout is located at road marker T-24 (2.5 miles west of Tenaya Lake and just slightly more than 2 miles east of the May Lake turnoff). Here the enormity of the granite walls of Tenaya Canyon is revealed, and unique views of Half Dome and Clouds Rest are allowed. To the east, the landscape includes Tenaya Lake and the many domes and peaks of the Tuolumne Meadows region. A short nature trail leads down from the point, and watch for fat and sassy marmots in the rocks (but please don't feed them).

**Q:** How did Gin Flat (about 5 miles west of Crane Flat on the Tioga Road) get its name?

**A:** Reportedly, a barrel of gin fell off a freight wagon, unmissed by the driver. It was found by a bunch of cowboys, sheepherders, and roadworkers who got "ginned up."

## Seven Sensational Hikes from the Tioga Road

**1. Harden Lake.** This is a relatively flat three-mile walk to an attractive little lake that offers picnicking, swimming, and fishing. Start in front of the White Wolf Campground and head north on what was the original Tioga Road. You can follow the road all the way to the lake or catch a trail branching off about a mile from it. If you take the road, bear to the right when it forks. There's a good view of the Tuolumne River Canyon from the far side of the lake. The round trip is about 6 miles and should take about 4 hours.

**2. Lukens Lake.** It's mostly uphill, but this hike of less than a mile terminates at a lovely spot amid meadow flowers and grasses. Being so close to the road, Lukens Lake is perfect for families with young (but not infant) children. Take your fishing poles and a picnic lunch. The trailhead is found 1.8 miles to the east of the White Wolf intersection; it's also 3 miles west of the spot where the Tioga Road crosses Yosemite Creek. Head north up the hill, then drop down to the lake. This easy hike is not quite two miles up and back, and requires about an hour to cover (a little longer for families!). You can also reach Lukens Lake from White Wolf. Ask for trail directions at the lodge.

**3. Yosemite Creek to Yosemite Valley.** From the point on the Tioga Road where it crosses Yosemite Creek (about 5 miles east of the White Wolf turn-off), a trail leads southward over level and downhill terrain all the way to Yosemite Valley. Because it's a one-way hike of 13 miles, you'll have to arrange for a ride to the trail-head, plan on shuttling back to pick up your car on the Tioga Road, or use the "Hiker's Bus" mentioned on page 61. The trail follows Yosemite Creek down to Yosemite Creek Campground and eventually to the top of Yosemite Falls. Check out the spectacular view from the top (see page 33) before descending the final 3.5 miles to the Yosemite Valley floor. This is a strenuous hike for the physically fit. Allow at least 8 hours for this demanding but satisfying trip.

**4. North Dome.** This difficult hike to one of the best views of Yosemite Valley (see page 39) takes off to the south of the Tioga Road at road marker T-19, about 5 miles beyond the point where the road crosses Yosemite Creek (this is also 2 miles west of the May Lake turn-off and just east of Porcupine Flat Campground). The walk is mostly downhill and flat for 4.2 miles to the dome. Watch for the erratic boulders left by the glaciers here, and check out the impressive view of Half Dome directly across from you. Because the return trip to the Tioga Road is mostly uphill, this should be considered a strenuous hike. Give yourself 6 to 8 hours for the 8.5-mile trip out and back.

**5. May Lake and Mount Hoffmann.** For those who like to get in the middle of things, Mount Hoffmann is the geographic center of Yosemite National Park. It offers superb views of the park's high country from its 10,850-foot summit. The trail up the mountain leads past idyllic May Lake, a beautiful spot and location of one of the High Sierra Camps (see page 64). Start your hike at the May Lake parking area. Turn north off the Tioga Road about 5 miles west of Tenaya Lake at road marker T-21 and drive 2 miles to the parking lot. It's an easy mile and a quarter to May Lake, and if you're adventurous, the 2 miles beyond to the top of Mount Hoffmann are considerably more strenuous but worth the effort (you will gain about 1,500 feet in elevation). Plan on 2 hours round trip for May Lake, and add 3 to 4 more for the ascent of Mount Hoffmann.

## 6. Mono Pass.

This high elevation hike is a comparatively easy four miles with an elevation gain of only 1,000 feet. The route, however, begins at nearly 10,000 feet and almost reaches the 11,000-foot level (prepare for some heavy breathing). The trail begins 1.5 miles west of Tioga Pass at road marker T-37, and heads south along an old Indian trading route. At Mono Pass itself are the remains of several mining buildings and cabins that were used during the late 1800s. Views of Mt. Gibbs and Mt. Dana are extremely fine. This 8-mile round trip should take from 4 to 6 hours depending upon your level of conditioning.

## 7. Gaylor Lakes.

Here's another trip for high-elevation freaks who love to huff and puff. The trail ascends steeply to the north from just a few feet west of the Tioga Pass Entrance Station that's 9,945 feet high. Middle Gaylor Lake is about a mile from the trailhead, but it's no easy climb. Follow the inflowing creek to Upper Gaylor Lake and the remnants of a stone shelter at the Great Sierra Mine 300 yards to its north. This is truly an alpine environment with few trees, strong winds, and often harsh weather. Allow 3 hours for this moderately difficult hike of 4 miles round trip.

**Q:** How should a hiker behave in a lightning storm?

**A:** Stay clear of open expanses of water, keep off open areas of rock and out of meadows, and stay away from prominent landmarks like lone, isolated trees. Seek shelter from the storm; a dense stand of trees of roughly the same height works well.

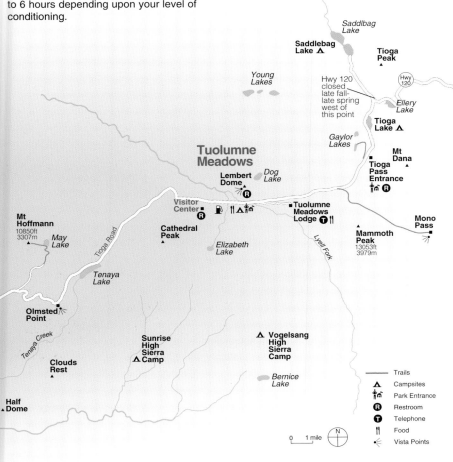

## The High Sierra Camps

Six rustic colonies of tents in the park's loftier regions constitute an institution unique to Yosemite called the High Sierra Camps. Placed in a roughly circular pattern about one day's hike apart, the camps allow visitors to enjoy high-elevation backcountry in semi-luxury. The semi-luxury aspect of the operation includes wholesome hot meals prepared by the camp staff, and regulation beds with mattresses, pillows, woolen blankets, and comforters that await weary travelers. There are even showers!

The idea for the camps was that of Washington B. Lewis, Yosemite's first NPS Superintendent. He wanted hikers to enjoy Yosemite's high country free from the "irksome" load of equipment and food normally needed for a backcountry trip. In 1924, the first camps were installed at a number of locations (several of which already had unofficial "High Sierra Camps"), and the system was underway.

Over the years there have been as many as eight different camp sites (including Little Yosemite Valley, Boothe Lake, Lyell Canyon, and Tenaya Lake), but the present configuration of six has been set for quite some time. The camps are open for a very short season (roughly late June or early July to Labor Day), and are operated by DNC Parks & Resorts at Yosemite.

The only camp accessible by road is the Tuolumne Lodge (see page 71). Many people use it as a starting or ending point for the High Sierra Loop Trip. In a clockwise direction from Tuolumne Meadows the other camps are Vogelsang, Merced Lake, Sunrise, May Lake, and Glen Aulin. The distance between each averages nine miles.

Guests at the High Sierra Camps are accommodated in dormitory-style tents that sleep either four or six. The communal bathhouses offer running water, showers, and toilets. Guests must provide their own sheets or sleep-sacks and towels. Hearty breakfasts and dinners are served daily, and bag lunches can be ordered. Sizes of the camps vary, but about 35 people on average can be lodged.

A favorite of many High Sierra Camp users is the 7-day guided loop trip (there's also a 4-day option). A maximum of 14 persons is accompanied by a naturalist who provides ongoing interpretation of the geology and natural history of Yosemite's wilderness. Campfire programs occur nightly, and members of the group develop a real spirit of camaraderie and friendship.

The High Sierra Camps are tremendously popular. Despite the price ($109 plus tax per night, including breakfast and dinner), the camps are fully booked almost every night of the summer. Reservations are essential and are handled by lottery. Applications are accepted each year between October 15 and December 15 for the lottery that is held in mid-December. Applicants will be notified by February 28 as to their standing in the lottery. For an application or more information write to the High Sierra Desk, Yosemite Reservations, 5410 E. Home Avenue, Fresno, CA 93727, or call (559) 253-5674, Monday through Friday from 8 a.m. to 5 p.m., and Saturday and Sunday from 8 a.m. to 3 p.m. (Pacific time).

## Tuolumne Meadows

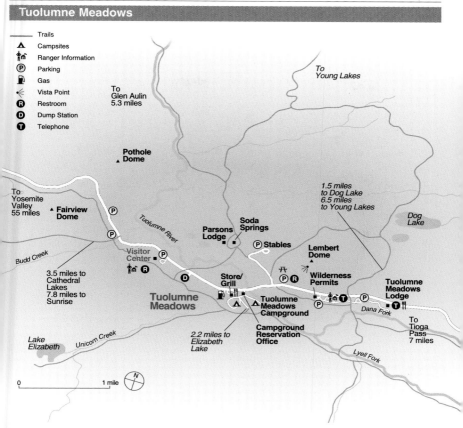

**Legend:**
- Trails
- ▲ Campsites
- Ranger Information
- Ⓟ Parking
- Gas
- Vista Point
- Ⓡ Restroom
- Ⓓ Dump Station
- Ⓣ Telephone

*The Tuolumne Meadow is a beautiful grassy plain of great extent, thickly enameled with flowers, and surrounded with the most magnificent scenery.*
—Joseph LeConte

This stunningly picturesque region sits 8,600 feet up in the transparent sky of Yosemite's high country. Contained in a basin about 2.5 miles long, the meadow system may be the largest in the Sierra Nevada at the subalpine level. Tuolumne Meadows is only 55 miles by road from Yosemite Valley, but it's a world apart.

Called by some the "hub" or "heart" of the high country, Tuolumne is a seasonal phenomenon. It is closed by snow to visitation the bulk of year, but when summer comes, the action is impressive. Hikers flock here, both daytrippers and backpackers. Rock climbers who winter in Yosemite Valley adopt Tuolumne as a summer home. And visitors in their cars arrive to revel in the awesome beauty of the place, and to enjoy a less-developed part of the park.

There's plenty to gawk at, too. The Tuolumne River winds its way sinuously through the meadows, while an array of unusually-shaped domes rings the area. There are smooth-bottomed canyons and jagged peaks; delicate lakes and odorous springs. These multiple elements combine to create a landscape both wonderful and inspiring.

During the summer months there's a ranger station at Tuolumne Meadows operated by the National Park Service along with a small visitor's center. The ranger station is just off the Tioga Road along the road to Tuolumne Lodge, and the Visitor's Center is located near the half-way point of the meadows about a quarter-mile west of the gas station and store. For information or assistance call 372-0263 or 372-4450.

**Further Reading**
*Map & Guide to Tuolumne Meadows* by Steven P. Medley. San Francisco, Rufus Graphics, 1994.

**Q:** What is the final destination of the water in the Tuolumne River that flows through Tuolumne Meadows?

**A:** The water is captured at Hetch Hetchy Reservoir and eventually ends up in the domestic water system of the City of San Francisco.

## Activities at Tuolumne

### Climb A Dome

Scrambling to the top of one of Tuolumne's granite domes can be fun and exhilarating. It can also be hazardous to your health. Try one of the easier rocks like Lembert Dome (see the hiking section below) or Pothole Dome (adjacent to the road at the west end of the meadows). Wear proper footgear and don't go up anything you aren't sure you can get down. Climbing lessons are available from the Mountaineering School in Tuolumne Meadows. Call 372-8435 for details and rates.

*Tuolumne River*

### Take A Swim

Because they are fed by the melting snow nearby, most of the streams, rivers, and lakes of the Tuolumne region are freezing cold. As the summer progresses, they warm a bit, but swimming is not for the weak of heart. There are plenty of good swimming holes along the Tuolumne River as it passes the campground, and on its fork that winds lazily through Lyell Canyon (see hiking section below). Lake swimmers should try Tenaya Lake, 7 miles to the west, Elizabeth Lake, or Dog Lake (both described below).

### Become A Sheepwatcher

In 1986, a small herd of California big-horn sheep was transplanted to the park in the Tioga Pass region. The sheep are native to the park, but were eliminated here by disease and hunting before 1900. The introduced herd leads a precarious existence (the sheep are particularly vulnerable to mountain lion predation), but is still considered viable. In recent summers there have been reports of bighorn sightings in the Tuolumne Meadows area. Check at the Visitor's Center for information and directions.

### Get Tall in the Saddle

Riding horses are stabled at Tuolumne Meadows by DNC Parks & Resorts at Yosemite each summer. As is the case throughout the park, they offer 2-hour, half-day, and all-day guided horseback trips. The Tuolumne stables can be found by turning north at road marker T-32 that is just east of the bridge over the Tuolumne River near the campground. For more information and rates call (209) 372-8427.

### Walk a Mile in Your Shoes

The hiking around Tuolumne Meadows is first-rate. The trails are varied, the scenery is exceptional, and the weather usually cooperative (but plan for afternoon thunder showers, particularly in August). A person staying at Tuolumne could take a different hike every day for a week and still not exhaust the possibilities. Be sure to follow normal hiking precautions (see page 30) and drink extra liquids to keep yourself hydrated at this high elevation

A free shuttle bus runs between Tuolumne Meadows and Tenaya Lake from July 1 through Labor Day. It's a good way to get to your trailhead and leave your car behind. Hours are posted on signs at bus stops throughout the Tuolumne area.

The DNC hiker's bus visits Tuolumne Meadows from Yosemite Valley once a day from July 1 through Labor Day. You can be dropped off at the trailhead of your choice and, if the timing works out, be picked up later. Call 372-1240 for information.

### Get Centered

To learn more about the Tuolumne Meadows region, visit the Visitor Center located south of the Tioga Road a short ways west of the gas station. There you'll find exhibits, knowledgeable rangers, and books and maps for sale. It's also a good place to find out about free ranger walks and programs that will be happening during your visit (or check the *Yosemite Guide*).

Children can participate in the Junior Ranger program by purchasing a copy of the *Junior Ranger Handbook* (ages 3-6) or the *Little Cub Handbook* (for children ages 7-13) at the center. By completing the activities outlined in the handbook, they can earn certificates and badges while they learn lots more about the park. The handbooks are available at all park visitors centers; in Tuolumne call 372-0263.

### Do Something Fishy

Tuolumne Meadows is loaded with family fishing opportunities. These high country trout seem to be plentiful, but they're small. Your kids will find the many rivers and lakes great places to practice their angling techniques. The Tuolumne River and its tributaries are excellent spots as are Dog Lake, Cathedral Lake, and Elizabeth Lake. Follow park fishing regulations (see page 29), and check at the Visitor Center for information or tips.

## Seven Scintillating Hikes from Tuolumne Meadows

**1. Cathedral Lakes.** Taking off from the obvious parking at the west end of Tuolumne Meadows (south of the road), this trail is fairly strenuous gaining about 1,000 feet in under 4 miles. The route is uphill, then relatively flat for a ways, then uphill again before it drops into the Cathedral Lakes basin. Take the right fork in the trail to reach the lower lake, which is the larger of the two. Have a swim, enjoy your lunch, or fish a little. Your view of Cathedral Peak will be outstanding. The round-trip hike is less than 8 miles and should take 4 to 6 hours.

**2. Elizabeth Lake.** It's steep and short and well worth the effort. Elizabeth Lake is a lovely spot nestled against the base of Unicorn Peak, one of Tuolumne's most recognizable landmarks. The 2.3-mile hike begins at the back side of the Tuolumne Meadows Campground (across from the bathrooms for the group camp area), and is just about all uphill. Given the elevation (you climb to about 9,500 feet), it's a good idea to take your time and adopt a slow but steady pace. The water's cold though swimmable, and fishing is fair. Allow from 3 to 4 hours for the 4.6-mile round trip.

**3. Soda Springs.** Here's an easy hike that's flat and perfect for all ages. The trail leads out into the middle of Tuolumne Meadows and to a naturally-carbonated mineral spring that bubbles mysteriously to the surface. Park in the parking lot just north of the Tioga Road at marker T-32 (just east of the bridge over the Tuolumne River near the campground) adjacent to Lembert Dome. Follow the gravel road to the north, and where the road turns right, walk around the brown metal gate and continue north (if you get to the stables, you're off route). Besides the Soda Springs, you'll find Parsons Memorial Lodge (erected in 1914 by the Sierra Club), and the McCauley Cabin, a pioneer structure now used as a ranger residence. You'll be close to the river and will get a sense of the size and beauty of the meadows. You can make the mile and a half walk in an hour.

*Iron deposits in Soda Springs*

**4. Glen Aulin.** To reach this aspen-studded hollow along the Tuolumne River, walk to Soda Springs (see above for hike information). The trail continues past the springs and roughly follows the river 7 miles to a small campground and one of the High Sierra Camps (see page 64). The trail is slightly downhill all the way, and that makes the hike back a stiff one. Watch for Tuolumne Falls and White Cascade as you hike. If you are truly a glutton for hiking punishment, Waterwheel Falls, one of the park's most unusual cascades, is 3.3 miles past Glen Aulin. The trip to Glen Aulin is a very strenuous hike of 14 miles round trip; give yourself 8 to 10 hours to accomplish it.

**5. Lembert Dome.** From the top of this oddly-shaped dome the 360 degree panorama of Tuolumne Meadows is fantastic. Start at the parking lot at the rock's base located north of the Tioga Road at marker T-32 (just east of the Tuolumne River). Don't start climbing here; follow the nature trail and leave it at marker #2. Climb steeply up the back side of the formation and make your way to the top. Take your topo map for identification of the many peaks and mountains around you. Up and back is about 2.8 miles and should require 3 hours of your time.

**6. Dog Lake.** This easily-reached spot is perfect for swimming, but not for fishing (there is a rumor that no fish remain within it). The hardest part of this 1.5-mile hike is finding the trailhead. At the east end of Tuolumne Meadows turn onto the road that leads to Tuolumne Lodge. Past the ranger station but before the lodge is a parking lot on the left side of the road. Park there, walk up the bank to the north, carefully cross the main road, and begin your hike up the hill. The trail is steep at first, then levels off for a final gradual ascent to the lake. A moderate hike of three miles round trip; allow 4 hours.

**7. Lyell Canyon.** This hike is the proverbial stroll in the park. The trail follows the Lyell Fork of the Tuolumne River out through the beautiful canyon that shares its name. The trailhead is at the west end of the parking lot for Tuolumne Lodge, but park your car in the lot for the Dog Lake hike. Head into the forest, cross a bridge, then continue to double bridges over the Lyell Fork (less than half a mile out). You leave the river at this point and follow the trail, which rejoins the river further out the canyon. It's a flat hike the entire route and as scenic and relaxing as they come. Lyell Canyon is about 8 miles long and you can hike as little or as much as you like. Give yourself enough time to make it back before dark.

## Camping North of Yosemite Valley

The campgrounds at the north end of the park can be characterized as more primitive and remote and generally smaller (with Tuolumne Meadows Campground being the main exception). Only a few are handled by the NPRS reservation system, and the balance are operated on a first-come, first-served basis. For campgrounds that can't be reserved in advance, remember that the check out time is noon; this is the perfect hour to attempt to secure a site.

Pets are not allowed in many campgrounds. Check the listings below to see if you can legally bring your pet, and always indicate that you'll be camping with a pet when you make your NPRS reservation. See page 12 for the specifics of dealing with NPRS and successfully arranging a campsite reservation.

There are also NPRS offices at the Big Oak Flat Entrance (where Highway 120 enters the park from the west) and in Tuolumne Meadows (at the entrance to the campground). At times campsites can be arranged at the last minute by stopping at one of these offices. Call 379-2123 for the Big Oak Flat NPRS and 372-0384 for the Tuolumne Office.

The summer camping limit is 14 days outside of Yosemite Valley, and most of the campgrounds are open only in the summer. The limit extends to 30 days the rest of the year, but you may only camp in Yosemite a total of 30 days in any one calendar year. For general park camping regulations, see page 34.

### Hetch Hetchy Area Campgrounds

**Crane Flat Campground:** This camping area of 166 sites is situated at the 6,200-foot level where the Big Oak Flat and Tioga Roads meet. Of all the campgrounds located outside Yosemite Valley, it's the closest – only 17 miles away. The nightly fee is $18, and NPRS reservations are required. Normally open from June through September, Crane Flat is close to the Merced and Tuolumne Big Tree Groves and the Toga Road attractions. Pets are allowed.

**Hodgdon Meadow Campground:** Here is the first place to camp when you enter Yosemite from the west on Highway 120 (you'll be 25 miles from Yosemite Valley). All types of campers are welcome in this campground consisting of 105 sites. To reach Hodgdon Meadow, turn down the hill just south of the Big Oak Flat Entrance. It's less than a half-mile to the campground entrance. NPRS reservations are required between May and September ($18 per site); the rest of the year, it's a first-come, first-served facility ($12 per site). Pets are allowed.

**Q:** Where did Hodgdon Meadow get its name?

**A:** It's named for Jeremiah Hodgdon, a Vermont native, who homesteaded the area in 1865.

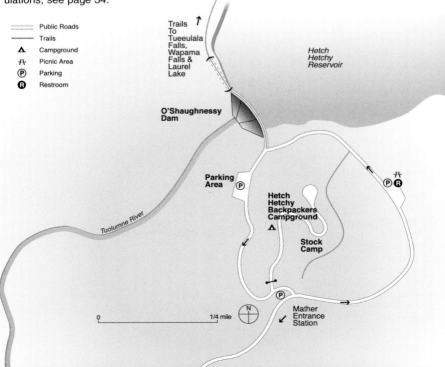

## Hetch Hetchy Backpackers Campground:

This relatively new campground is exclusively for backpackers and other backcountry users (with wilderness permits) who are beginning their trips from the Hetch Hetchy trailhead. Stays are limited to one night at the beginning and end of wilderness outings. Located at Hetch Hetchy Reservoir, the campground features 19 backpacker sites (6 persons per site), 2 organized group sites (one accommodating 18 persons, the other 25), and 2 stock use sites (6 persons and 6 head of stock per site). Parking is provided near the campground, which has running water and flush toilets. No recreational vehicles, trailers, or pets are allowed. Prior arrangements should be made for the organized group and stock use sites. The fees are $5 per night for backpackers and $35 per site for the group and stock sites. Write to the Mather District Office, Star Route, Groveland, CA 95321 or call 372-0323.

### Tioga Road Campgrounds

**Tamarack Flat Campground:** If you enjoy a more primitive camping experience (creek water that must be boiled and pit toilets), this campground fits the bill. It's located at 6,300 feet down a three-mile dirt road that takes off the Tioga Road about 4 miles east of Crane Flat (not suitable for large recreational vehicles or trailers). There are 52 campsites, the fee is $8 per night, and it's handled on a first-come, first-served basis. Usually open between June and September. No pets.

**White Wolf Campground:** A favorite of many high country campers, White Wolf is set on a beautiful meadow alongside a bubbling creek. Added amenities are the White Wolf Lodge with a small store and restaurant, and public showers for a fee. The 8,000-foot setting 14 miles east of Crane Flat makes for cold nights and brilliant days. There are 74 first-come, first-served sites which rent for $12 per night (not suitable for RVs over 27 feet long). The camping season here is approximately July through September. Pets are allowed.

**Yosemite Creek Campground:** Another primitive campground, the Yosemite Creek camping area is located 5 miles down a narrow dirt road to the south of the Tioga Road (the turnoff is less than a half-mile east of the White Wolf turn-off). Don't, repeat don't, even think about trying to take an RV or a trailer into this campground. The 75 sites utilize pit toilets and water from nearby Yosemite Creek (be sure to treat it). First-come, first-served, $8 per night, and open July through September only. Pets are allowed.

## Porcupine Flat Campground:

They call it a flat campground, but there are flatter campgrounds in the world. There is no running water and no flush toilets here, but Porcupine Creek wanders by and the lodgepole pines make a fine canopy. Because the roads in the campground are very bad, recreational vehicles are limited to a few campsites at the entry to the campground; there are 52 sites total. The fee is $8 per night for these first-come, first-served sites. Open usually from July through September; no pets are allowed.

### Tuolumne Meadows Campgrounds

**Tuolumne Meadows Campground:** Here is the park's largest single campground with 304 sites. The road complex throughout the area is complicated and confusing, but once you get the hang of it, you'll love this campground. Families return here year after year for the camping, fishing, hiking, and scenery. NPRS reservations are required for half the camp sites, the balance are handled on a first-come, first-served basis. There's a store nearby, a restaurant and showers for a fee at Tuolumne Lodge, horseback riding at the stables, and fishing in the adjacent Tuolumne River. A sanitary dump station is also available. Backpackers and visitors without vehicles may take advantage of 25 walk-in sites for a fee of $5 per night, with a one night maximum stay. Regular sites rent for $18 per night, and the camp is kept open from July through September in a typical year. Pets are allowed.

**Tuolumne Group Campground:** Special campsites within this campground are available for organized groups by prior arrangement. Reservations should be in advance with NPRS (see page 12). Each site, for tent camping only, can accommodate no fewer than 13 and no more than 35 people. No pets are allowed. For more information, call 372-0402.

## Gas, Food & Lodging North of Yosemite Valley

### Gas

There are two Chevron gas stations in the north portion of Yosemite: one at Crane Flat and the other at Tuolumne Meadows. Only the Crane Flat station is open year round. If you are traveling the Tioga Road, be sure to check your gas gauge as it's a stretch of almost 40 miles where no services are provided. Major credit cards are accepted. Check the *Yosemite Today* for hours of operation. A repair garage is open all year in Yosemite Valley, and towing service can be arranged 24 hours a day by calling 372-8320.

### Food: Restaurants

The north end of the park is relatively undeveloped. Visitors looking for fine restaurants and haute cuisine should try San Francisco or Los Angeles. While there are a few options for hearty meals in generally rustic facilities, you should plan on picnicking a lot and preparing your own food when you travel to Yosemite's north country. The following is a list of your choices (open only during the visitor season of June through October) should you choose to "dine out." Check the *Yosemite Today* for dates and hours of operation.

**Evergreen Lodge:** Not technically within the park, this old wooden lodge is 7 miles out Evergreen Road on the way to Hetch Hetchy. The simple dining room and unpretentious bar exude an unpolished charm, and at last check, the food was remarkably good. They serve dinner 7 nights a week and breakfast on weekends (lunch items are available at the small store on premises). The Evergreen Lodge is not listed in the *Yosemite Guide*, so call (209) 379-2606 for information on times of operation and to make a reservation. Their normal season is from April through October. Moderate to expensive prices.

**White Wolf Lodge:** With its covered porch and its low-key yet intimate dining room, the White Wolf Lodge, a whitewashed wooden structure, is an enjoyable spot to eat. Breakfast and dinner are served from a menu inside (grab a table on the porch if they're serving outdoors), and box lunches can be ordered and sandwiches and other items can be purchased from the adjacent store. There's a fine old fireplace, adequate food, and beer and wine. When you consider that the staff gets spread pretty thin with their multiple duties, the service is fine. Dinner reservations are recommended; call 372-8416. Moderate to expensive.

**Tioga Pass Resort:** Here's another spot that fails to qualify as a "park" establishment because it's two miles beyond the Tioga Pass Entrance on Forest Service land. But the place is a Yosemite institution and had to be included. They serve breakfast, lunch, and dinner in a room so small that many times you'll be asked to wait for long periods before you can be seated. The wait is worth it, however; try the homemade pies, delicious sandwiches, and substantial breakfasts. Get a load of the classic water spigot with rock-lined drain that's from some other era, and the wonderful curved counter. Recently they've added an outdoor coffee bar for those in quest of caffeine. For reservations, hours, or information, call (209) 372-4471. Moderate prices.

*Tuolumne Lodge*

**Tuolumne Meadows Lodge:** The lodge is one of the six High Sierra Camps in Yosemite (see page 64) and the only one accessible by automobile. The dining room is located in a canvas-sided tent-like structure that captures the feeling of roughing it in the high country. But the food will make you think you're someplace fancy. Breakfast and dinner are served from a menu family style; that is, you get seated with whomever happens to be present for mealtime when you are. It's good fun, and many fast friendships have been initiated in the lodge dining room. Beer and wine are served, and box lunches are available upon request. Dinner reservations are required and can be made by calling 372-8413. Moderate to expensive prices.

**Tuolumne Meadows Grill:** Located adjacent to theTuolumne store and post office, the grill is a great place for a hamburger. The service is as fast as you'll get anywhere, and they pour a big cup of coffee. Pull up a stool or stand and wolf. Fry-cooked meals are served at breakfast, lunch, and dinner (but the Lodge is preferred for breakfast if you're in no hurry). No reservations accepted (it's not that kind of place), and you can order menu items "to go." Inexpensive prices

## Food: Groceries

The following outlets are basic convenience stores with limited selections. Check the *Yosemite Today* for operating hours.

**Crane Flat Gas Station:** Located in the main building of the Chevron station at the intersection of the Big Oak Flat and Tioga Roads. Phone 379-2349.

**White Wolf Lodge:** A very small camp store adjacent to the dining room at the lodge. Phone 372-8416.

**Tuolumne Meadows Store:** This facility offers the largest selection and variety north of Yosemite Valley. Phone 372-8428.

## Lodging

As in the Wawona area, there are overnight accommodations in the north part of the park that are not operated by DNC Parks & Resorts at Yosemite. For reservations for DNC facilities, follow the steps outlined on page 11. You must deal directly with the other independent lodging providers to reserve with them.

The quoted rates for the following listed lodging facilities are approximate only, are based on double occupancy, vary with the seasons, and are subject to change.

**Evergreen Lodge:** Open April through October. Here are 18 rustic cabins on the road to Hetch Hetchy. One bedroom cabins are $99-139, one bedroom cottages are $139-159, and two bedroom family cabins are $159-189. Each cabin includes a private bath, but there are no kitchens. Other amenities are a restaurant, bar, and small convenience store. For reservations call directly to (800) 935-6343 or 379-2606. The web site address is www.evergreenlodge.com.

**White Wolf Lodge:** Open in summer only. These rustic accommodations are situated at delightful White Wolf, bordered by meadow and forest both. There are four cabins with private bath (about $87) featuring propane heating, a desk, chair, dresser, and two double beds. Limited electricity is provided for lighting and heat. The 24 canvas tent cabins share a com-

*Tioga high country*

munal bathroom and shower house (about $67). The canvas cabins are equipped with beds with linens, candles for lighting, a wood burning stove, and wood. There is no electricity. Special amenities include a dining room and store. Reservations should be made through DNC (see page 11).

**Tioga Pass Resort:** Open Memorial Day through mid-October. Nestled on the side of a hill at well over the 9,000-foot level, the resort consists of 10 housekeeping cabins, 4 motel-type rooms, and a central building with restaurant, store, and gas pumps. A new addition is the outdoor coffee bar. It's two miles beyond Tioga Pass Entrance and just outside of the park. Room rates vary from $100 to $175 per night. Weekly rates are offered. For reservations write PO Box 7, Lee Vining, CA 93541, or call 372-4471. The web site address is www.tiogapassresort.com.

**Tuolumne Meadows Lodge:** Open in summer only. Here are 69 canvas tent cabins set close by the Tuolumne River in a picture book setting. The tents are rustic and utilize wood stoves and candles (there's no electricity), but there are mattresses and linen on the beds. Bathrooms and showers are communal and anything but fancy. But that's part of the fun of the Tuolumne Lodge—it's roughing it easy. The tents rent for about $71 and will sleep up to 4. Reservations (which are much sought and highly coveted) should be made through DNC (see page 11).

Inexpensive: dinner for one adult might cost up to $10. Moderate: dinner for one adult might cost from $10 to $20. Expensive: dinner for one adult might cost over $20.

*Hikers on Mt. Dana*

# Yosemite's Natural World

Yosemite is filled with living things of every description existing in a remarkable setting created by the various forces of nature. From its famous black bears and big trees to nocturnal owls, seldom-seen reptiles, pesky mosquitos, and mysterious fungi, the park is abundant with flora and fauna that are rich and varied. Because wildlife is protected in Yosemite, it has served as an "island" sanctuary of sorts, where natural processes have continued and biological diversity is still great. Other factors contributing to this favorable situation for animals and plants are the great range of elevations within the park (from 2,000 feet to 13,000 feet) and the corresponding variety of living conditions that change with the elevation.

Though inanimate, other natural objects and processes contribute to the ever-evolving Yosemite scene. Geological workings are constant, waterfalls ebb and flow, and meteorological forces add variety and life to the landscape. And because the setting has been so unchanged and undeveloped, Yosemite National Park is even more significant as a mountain laboratory of the natural world.

## Yosemite Geology for Liberal Arts Majors

*M*ost descriptions of Yosemite geology are rife with technical jargon, geological gobbledy gook, and scientific names. This is an attempt to make the processes that created Yosemite's landscape of granite and water more understandable for the layperson. And with it comes the promise that words like batholith, pyroclastic, and subduction will not be used.

Once upon a time about 500 million years ago, sediment was deposited in layers on the ocean floor at the west edge of what would later become the continent of North America. This sediment was consolidated into rocks like sandstone, chert, shale, and limestone. Neither the land mass of the developing continent nor the land mass covered by sedimentary rock under the ocean was stationary, however.

Time passed (about 300 million years or so) and the two land masses moved towards each other, met, and then some exciting geology took place. The rock beneath the ocean was forced under the continental land mass with interesting results. The process caused the rock of the ocean plate to become very hot and liquefy into magma (which is the molten rock that shoots out of volcanoes). This hot liquid rose up under the edge of the continent to form volcanoes, and where it cooled and hardened before making it to the surface, great areas of granite rock.

This process occurred in a series of pulses over a period of some 150 million years. When it was complete, a mountain range had been formed that ran in a rough line parallel to the west coast. Although it was largely covered by the continental crust (primarily sedimentary rock), this ancestral Sierra Nevada range was probably similar to the present Cascade Range of volcanoes. In some places the mountains may have been as high as 13,000 feet.

For approximately the next 55 million years, the main force at work in the ancestral Sierra was erosion (we all know what that is, right?). The volcanoes were worn away by wind and water as was the continental crust that sat on top of the great granite mass created by the molten rock as described above. The rock that eroded away was carried by rivers and streams into California's Central Valley. When this period of erosion was complete, what was to become the Sierra Nevada, now primarily exposed granite, stood only a few thousand feet high.

Everything was going along fine with the developing Sierra until one day about 25 million years ago, the land masses meeting along the present day San Andreas fault began to move again. The result was that the block upon which the Sierra sat was uplifted at its eastern edge and tilted towards the west. It is estimated that the tilt raised peaks on Yosemite's eastern edge as much as 11,000 feet.

Following uplift and tilt, river courses in the Yosemite region became steeper, and the erosive effect of their waters increased. The Merced River, for example, began to carve the granite much more sharply, and Yosemite Valley was deepened as a canyon. The Sierra Nevada began to show much greater surface relief, and started to take on the form we know today.

About 2 or 3 million years ago, the Earth's climate began to cool. Given its raised height, the Sierra Nevada became covered with glaciers and ice fields along its crest. At its most extensive, the ice covered over half of Yosemite, and sent glaciers down many of the valleys that had been created by the erosion of streams and rivers.

Glaciers tore loose large quantities of rock as they moved, carving U-shaped canyons and valleys, polishing rock faces, and breaking various rock formations like spires and domes along fractures or joints. The glaciers carried the broken rock as rubble and deposited it along the edges of its path.

This glacial period consisted of an unknown number of glaciations – perhaps as many as 10. The last glaciation reached its maximum between 20,000 and 15,000 years ago. At that point, the Earth's climate began to warm again, glaciers receded, and non-glacial erosion became the main geological force working in Yosemite once more.

Yosemite Valley is one location in the park that has changed its appearance considerably since glacial times. Because glaciers dumped enormous quantities of rock and rubble at its western end, the valley's outflow was stopped and its floor became covered with water. Lake Yosemite was formed. Over the intervening 10,000 years, the lake was filled with sediment and silt washed down from the park's higher regions, and the valley's flat, dry floor we know today was created.

**Q:** What is an erratic boulder?

**A:** A large rock that has been transported from a distant source by the action of glacial ice. (Look for erratics on Yosemite's peaks and ridges.)

Yosemite's landscape continues to change even now. While the geological processes are not dramatic (some changes take millions of years), erosion continues, avalanches occur, and rockslides are common. The geologic story goes on in Yosemite and provides us with a better understanding of the extraordinary scenery that has made the park famous.

*Erratic boulders*

## Further Reading

*The Geologic Story of Yosemite National Park* by N. King Huber. Yosemite NP: Yosemite Associaton, 1989.

*Domes, Cliffs & Waterfalls* by William R. Jones. Yosemite NP: Yosemite Association, 1976.

*The Geology of the Sierra Nevada* by Mary Hill. Berkeley: University of California Press, 1975.

*The Incomparable Valley* by Francois E. Matthes. Berkeley: University of California Press, 1950

## Geologists Disagree: Muir vs. Whitney

Nineteenth-century scientists were as puzzled by Yosemite Valley's origin as many first-time visitors are today. Their efforts to explain what they saw resulted in a variety of theories about the creation of the valley's sheer walls and spectacular waterfalls.

Josiah D. Whitney was the State Geologist for California and Director of the California Geological Survey and made many of the first studies of Yosemite during the 1860s. In his view, Yosemite Valley had not been formed by erosion or glaciation or any other traditional geologic force. He believed that a valley so deep could only have been created by a sudden, catastrophic collapse of that section of the earth below it. Because Whitney was an accomplished Harvard professor with quite a reputation as a scholar and scientist, his theory gained some acceptance.

At about the same time, mountain wanderer John Muir (see page 108) was making observations of his own. He, too, was fascinated with the geologic history of Yosemite Valley. Muir advanced the hypothesis that it was the action of glaciers, an "over-sweeping ice current," that had carved the Yosemite landscape. He worked to popularize the theory and it came to be known as "Muir's discovery."

Whitney was not impressed nor convinced. He characterized Muir's ideas as absurd, and passed them off as the ravings of a "mere shepherd." Doggedly, Whitney defended his "cataclysm" theory for some twenty years until his death.

While Muir was not correct in all the details of the work of the glaciers, he was remarkably close. Later studies proved the basic soundness of this theory and helped establish John Muir's reputation as a thoughtful and insightful student of the Sierra.

### Joints Shaped the Rocks

The variety of rock shapes and formations that occur in Yosemite is impressive. From blocks to domes to spires to arches to sheets, there is tremendous diversity in the granitic terrain. How did these structures come to be?

All of Yosemite's unusual landmarks (with but a few exceptions) resulted from the existence of fractures within their original rock structures. These fractures, called joints, are the lines upon which the rocks have been broken. They create zones of weakness within the granite that yield to the action of glaciers and to the intrusion of water.

Joints occur both vertically and horizontally, and some are inclined (for example, the Three Brothers formation was created along inclined joints). Vertical jointing is most prevalent and produced features like the face of Half Dome and the Cathedral Spires. Where vertical and horizontal joints intersect, the result is rectangular blocks.

Half Dome and El Capitan are representative of rocks with very sparse jointing. Their resistance to erosion and glaciation has kept them practically unchanged for thousands of years. Incidentally, there probably is no other half of Half Dome. Geologists believe that only 20% of the dome's original size has been lost.

The type of jointing most dramatic in the evolution of the Yosemite landform is sheeting, that results in the concentric joints that lead to the creation of domes. How these joints form is fairly complicated, but they occur mainly with the unloading of the pressure from overlying rock. As relief is experienced, the granite expands upward and fractures result. The concentric fractures break off like the different layers of an onion in a process called exfoliation.

## Yosemite Waterfalls

The collection of waterfalls in Yosemite National Park is unequalled anywhere in the world. And nowhere else have so many spectacular waterfalls been concentrated in so small an area as Yosemite Valley. What's most remarkable is the number of park waterfalls that are free-leaping; they make their descent without being broken on intervening ledges or outcroppings. The park's glacial geology is directly responsible for this unique situation.

While the glaciers carved major water courses like Yosemite Valley very deeply, lateral tributary ice streams cut much more slowly and less effectively. The result was "hanging valleys," and streams and creeks which previously had fed directly into primary rivers became routed over the brinks of lofty precipices into the more deeply-carved canyons below them. These waters still leap into space over sheer walls as Yosemite's waterfalls today. Good examples of waterfalls originating from hanging valleys are Yosemite Falls and Bridalveil Fall.

Other waterfalls were created as the glaciers moved along and dislocated large blocks of granite from streambeds. The rock gave way along joints (pre-existing fractures where the rock was weak) and took on shapes like steps in a staircase. This was the process responsible for Vernal and Nevada Falls, which drop in two major steps from Little Yosemite Valley. Known as the "Giant Staircase," this landform is well viewed from Glacier Point.

*Tuolumne Falls*

Yosemite's waterfalls are at peak flow during the months of April, May, and June when 75% of the annual snow melt occurs. May is usually the best single month for waterfall watching. By July most of the surface runoff is gone, and many falls either dry up or are reduced to a trickle. Some falls rarely dry up because of watersheds with soils that are able to hold more water longer (for example, Bridalveil Fall).

Not all the waterfalls in the park are large, spectacular, or permanent. Many cascades exist where streambeds were resistant to the glaciers, but some gouging and polishing did occur. In those cases, channels were steepened, and now water spills

**Q:** What are ephemeral waterfalls?

**A:** They are minor waterfalls with small watersheds or falls created by stream flows originating in catch basins that have captured runoff or rainfall. They are characterized by their temporary duration. Examples in Yosemite Valley are Horsetail Fall (on El Capitan) and Staircase Fall below Glacier Point.

*Upper Yosemite Fall*

over irregularly-fractured granite or down gradual cliff faces. Other falls are ephemeral; they appear only during heavy thunder storms or at the peak of the spring runoff. As abruptly as the rain ends, so do these fleeting displays.

In winter, park waterfalls have a different beauty. Because the snow pack prevents soil moisture from freezing, water continues to flow in the falls. But they become edged with ice, and droplets of water actually freeze as they descend through space. When this freezing occurs in a large volume, frazil ice is the result. Streams at the base of the waterfalls become filled with ice crystals that create ice slush. As it moves, the frazil ice adheres to any object below freezing, and

*Ice cone*

can clog stream beds.

The most famous winter waterfall phenomenon is the ice cone that builds up at the base of Upper Yosemite Fall. As ice slabs that have frozen at the fall's edges fall and gently freezing spray collects, the ice cone grows, sometimes to a height of 300 feet covering some four acres. The cone usually melts away by April.

## Further Reading

*Granite, Water, and Light: Waterfalls of Yosemite Valley* by Michael Osborne. Yosemite NP: Yosemite Association, 1983 (currently out of print).

*The Waterfalls of Yosemite* by Steven P. Medley. Yosemite NP: Yosemite Association, 1999.

---

### The Spirits of Yosemite Falls - A Yosemite Miwok Legend

In the waters just below Cho'-lok (Yosemite Falls) live the Po'-loti, a group of dangerous spirit women. In the old days there was a village a short distance from the falls.

A maiden from this village went to the stream for a basket of water. She dipped the basket into the stream as usual, but brought it up full of snakes. She went further upstream and tried again, but with the same result. She tried repeatedly, each time a little farther upstream, but always drew a basketful of snakes.

Finally, she reached the pool at the foot of Cho'-lok, and a sudden, violent wind blew her into it.

During the night she gave birth to a child that she wrapped in a blanket and brought home the next morning. The girl's mother was very curious and soon took the blanket off the baby in order to see it.

Immediately a violent gale arose and blew the entire village and its inhabitants into the same pool. Nothing has ever been seen or heard of them since.

From *Legends of the Yosemite Miwok,* compiled by Frank LaPena, Craig D. Bates, and Steven P. Medley (Yosemite Association, 1993).

---

## The Ten Highest Free-falling Waterfalls in the World

| | | | |
|---|---|---|---|
| 1. | Angel Falls | 3,212 feet | Venezuela |
| 2. | Tugela Falls | 3,110 feet | South Africa |
| 3. | Utigordsfossen | 2,625 feet | Norway |
| 4. | Mongefossen | 2,540 feet | Norway |
| **5.** | **Yosemite Falls** | 2,425 feet | Yosemite |
| 6. | Espelandsfoss | 2,307 feet | Norway |
| 7 | Ostre Mardalsfossen | 2,149 feet | Norway |
| **8.** | **Sentinel Falls** | 2,000 feet | Yosemite |
| | Cuquenan Falls | 2,000 feet | Venezuela |
| 9. | Sutherland Falls | 1,904 feet | New Zealand |
| 10. | Kjellfossen | 1,841 feet | Norway |

## Waterfalls of Yosemite Valley

| | | |
|---|---|---|
| Yosemite Falls | 2,425 feet | North wall, eastern end |
| Sentinel Falls | 2,000 feet | South wall, west of Sentinel Rock |
| Ribbon Fall | 1,612 feet. | North wall, west of El Capitan |
| Staircase Falls | 1,300 feet | South wall, behind Curry Village |
| Royal Arch Cascade | 1,250 feet | North wall, west of Washington Column |
| Silver Strand Falls | 1,170 feet | South wall, far west end |
| El Capitan Falls | 1,000 feet | North wall, east side of El Capitan |
| Lehamite Falls | uncertain | North wall, in Indian Canyon |
| Bridalveil Fall | 620 feet | South wall, west end |
| The Cascades | uncertain | North wall, 2 miles west of Yosemite Valley |
| Nevada Fall | 594 feet | Easternmost end of Merced River Canyon |
| Illilouette Fall | 370 feet | Panorama Cliffs southeast of Glacier Point |
| Vernal Fall | 317 feet | East of Happy Isles on Merced River |

## Natural Events

### Fires

Fire has long played a role in Yosemite's natural world. It is a major ecological force, with impacts similar to those of other natural phenomena, such as floods, earthquakes, and hurricanes. Wildland fires, defined as all fires that burn in natural environments, greatly influence park ecosystems. Prior to the appearance of humans here, the ingredients for fire were largely controlled by climate. With the arrival of Native Americans and later Euro-American settlers, sources of fire and fuels were modified as people changed their environment.

Wildland fire fosters new plant growth, expands wildlife populations, and removes dead trees and litter from the forest floor. Also, shrubs and trees invading grasslands and meadows are killed by fires. Following fire, new healthy re-growth occurs. Accordingly, fire is recognized as an instrument of change and a catalyst for promoting biological diversity and healthy ecosystems.

On occasion, wildfires (unwanted fires in the natural environment) originating in national parks burn forests, towns, or homes, with devastating results. Because of these negative impacts, people often mistakenly consider all fires to be harmful, destructive forces. However, properly managed fire, referred to as prescribed fire, can be an effective natural resource management tool.

In Yosemite, fires usually are classified as either natural or human-induced. A natural fire is usually started by lightning. Natural fires may burn under prescribed conditions and are monitored. Wildfires are those that humans seek to extinguish.

A prescribed fire is initiated by humans under predetermined conditions and is used to manage certain types of landscapes. These uses include reducing fuel build-up around campground areas or providing proper soil conditions for the germination of such species as the giant sequoia. Among the other benefits of prescribed burning are:

- insect pest control;

- removal of undesirable plants that compete with wanted species for nutrients;

- addition of nutrients for trees and other vegetation provided by ashes that remain after a fire;

- removal of undergrowth, thereby allowing sunlight to reach the forest floor to encourage growth of desirable species; and

- clearing of congested forest areas to prevent the accumulation of fuels.

**Note:** For more information see the National Park Service FireNet web site. at www.fire.nps.gov.

### The Fires of 1990

In August 1990, lightning from intense thunderstorms along the west side of Yosemite ignited about 40 different fires.

Because the fires threatened human life and property, park staff immediately began to suppress them.

But two of the fires, known as the A-Rock and the Steamboat, quickly grew to a size that was beyond control. A number of factors contributed to the severity of the fires, among them high winds, drought conditions, large amounts of available fuel, and steep terrain. The fires quickly advanced to become the most intense type, crown fires, which burn through the top layer of foliage on a tree, known as the canopy.

Containment and ultimate control of the two fires took some two weeks, more than 3,000 firefighters, and more than $13 million. The A-Rock fire eventually encompassed 18,100 acres, while the Steamboat fire covered about 5,280 acres. Damage was estimate at about $26 million, with the loss of homes (primarily in the park inholding known as Foresta) and concessioner and gateway community business income.

More than ten years later, the effects of the fires can still be seen. From the Big Oak Flat Road a few miles above Yosemite Valley, the Foresta region still appears starkly devoid of mature trees. While vegetation is slowly maturing, it will be many more years before some semblance of the area's previous coniferous forest returns. There are also stretches of the Wawona Road between Yosemite Valley and Chinquapin (the turn-off to Glacier Point) where many acres of burned forest are visible on both sides of the roadway.

## Floods

Since Yosemite was first occupied by those who wrote about their experiences, its natural water courses have flooded periodically. In 1862, homesteader James Lamon was forced from his home by the rising Merced River, and in 1958 the Wawona Covered Bridge was damaged by the waters of the South Fork.

History has shown that flooding by the Merced is not uncommon - rather it should be expected. Specifically, floods in Yosemite Valley occurred in 1937, 1950, 1955, 1963, 1980, and 1982. Such events were the result of various factors, but the most common was warm winter rains falling on accumulated snow up to the highest elevations of the park. When such conditions occur, huge quantities of run-off cannot be accommodated by the existing river channels, and water flows into meadows, forests, and developed areas.

Because of the relative regularity with which flooding occurs in Yosemite Valley, its flood plain has been carefully mapped. That map is now an integral part of the Yosemite Valley Plan that guides all future development of the valley. From now on, no more structures will be built within the flood plain in hopes that harm occasioned by high water to humans and their property will be minimized.

## The Flood of 1997

In the early morning hours of January 1, 1997, rain fell on packed snow in Yosemite at elevations up to 9,500 feet. The deluge from the storm combined with the huge amount of snow melted by the rain created a high volume of water rarely seen in the rivers and waterfalls of the park.

Run-off peaked in Yosemite Valley at about 11 p.m. on January 2, and streams and rivers there overflowed their banks and carved new channels. Over 2,000 people (employees and visitors alike) were initially stranded in the valley, when all three access highways were closed. After the water subsided, downed trees were removed, and road repairs were completed, evacuation was finally made.

The effects of the flood were wide-ranging. While the widening of water channels, scouring and erosion of riverbanks, and uprooting of trees and shrubs did occur, the flood's impact on the natural scene was not major. On the other hand, human-made structures and systems were seriously affected. Electrical service was shut down, mud and rock slides blocked roads and damaged power poles, sewer lines broke, and campgrounds, buildings, and roads were flooded. In some cases, large sections of roadway were washed away or had their underlying roadbeds destroyed.

While initial repairs and recovery efforts were being made, Yosemite Valley was closed to the public for three months. For the next two and one-half years, repairs to the Arch Rock Road and Highway 140 continued, requiring regular road closures; unrestricted access to Yosemite Valley was finally achieved again in October, 2000.

## 1997 Flood Statistics

- More than 1.4 miles of riverbank and 550 acres of meadows were eroded in Yosemite Valley.

- About half of Yosemite Valley's 900 campsites were flooded. Many have since been eliminated and are not likely to be replaced.

- Nine road bridges in the valley suffered damage and required repair. The bridge at Happy Isles has been removed.

- A 300-foot section of the 14-inch sewer line located beneath the Arch Rock Road was destroyed, severing the valley sewer system and contaminating the Merced River.

- Over 350 motel and cabin units at Yosemite Lodge were flooded and removed.

- Over 200 concession employee quarters were flooded, and 439 employees were displaced.

- At least ten archeological sites sustained heavy damage, with total removal of some cultural features and artifacts.

- The estimated cost of recovering from the damage and effects of the flood is $178,053,000.

## Yosemite Plantlife

There are over 1,500 different types of plants in Yosemite. They range from the grand sequoias to tiny fungi and lichen. What follows is a brief overview of Yosemite flora with information on how to find out much more.

### Trees

Both cone-bearing and broad-leaved trees appear in abundance within Yosemite National Park. The trees that bear cones (also known as conifers) do not shed all of their leaves or needles on an annual basis, and this has led to their designation as "evergreens." Most of the broad-leaved trees drop their leaves each year.

**The Conifers:** There are at least 18 different species of conifers that occur in the park. About half of them are pines. Most common at lower elevations are the ponderosa (or yellow) pine and the Jeffrey pine. The ponderosa is abundant in Yosemite Valley, has yellow-orange bark, needles in groups of three, bark scales that fit together like a jigsaw puzzle, and a trunk up to six feet in diameter. The Jeffrey pine looks much like the ponderosa but grows at higher elevations (Glacier Point is a typical locality). If in doubt, smell the bark. The Jeffrey exudes a sweet odor like vanilla or pineapple.

The two typical high-elevation pines are the lodgepole and the white bark. The lodgepole has needles in twos, yellowish bark, and small cones. The white bark features needles in bunches of five and purplish, pitchy cones, and tends to be dwarfed at tree line.

Other notable conifers are the red and white firs. Large forests of these trees can be seen along the Tioga and Glacier Point Roads. White firs occur between 3,500 and 8,000 feet and have 2-inch needles that twist off the branch and 3-to-5-inch cones. Red firs, in contrast, have shorter needles that curl upwards and larger cones (5 to 8 inches), and grow between 6,000 and 9,000 feet.

**Broad-Leaved Trees:** Almost without exception, these trees lose their leaves in the fall (they are deciduous). As the leaves die as part of this annual process, they take on different hues such as orange, yellow, and brown. It is the foliage of the broad-leaved trees, then, that provides us with sometimes spectacular "fall color." The deciduous trees are less varied than the conifers in the park.

There are many types of oaks in Yosemite. In the valley, the California black oak is distinctive. It grows to heights of 75 feet, has dark gray to black bark, and produces large acorns that the Yosemite Indians used as a staple in their diet. The other common oak is the canyon live oak, which has holly-like evergreen leaves.

*Mountain dogwood*

Other conspicuous broad-leaved trees are the mountain dogwood that produces beautiful and delicate whitish-green flowers each spring, and the quaking aspen known for its paper-thin white bark and the rustling of its often-colorful leaves with the slightest breeze.

Along streams and rivers, particularly at lower elevations, one will encounter cottonwoods (leaves are bright green on top and light below), willows (slender pointed leaves), and alders (dark green leaves with obvious veins and small teeth).

**Q:** What species are the large pine trees that sport long cones hanging from their upper branches like Christmas tree ornaments?

**A:** Sugar pine. Because the trees yield great quantities of even-grained, clear wood that is excellent for building, most of the forests of sugar pine in California were harvested during the nineteenth century.

*Sugar pine*

*Ponderosa pine*

## Flowering Plants

The spectacular geography of Yosemite, with its elevations ranging from 2,000 to over 13,000 feet, supports a natural wildflower garden without equal, not to mention shrubs, grasses, sedges, rushes, ferns, and fungi. The differing temperatures, precipitation levels, and growing seasons ensure that a wide assortment of plants finds conditions to their liking at locations throughout the park.

The blooming season is a long one in Yosemite. It starts in the foothills in April and May and gradually moves upslope as the weather warms and the snow melts. It doesn't reach the park's highest elevations until August, when flowers appear for a brief two-month appearance. All told, the wildflower season in Yosemite lasts a full six months!

For the student of botany, Yosemite is indeed a remarkable classroom. Within the park is some of the most distinctive vegetation in the world. Because natural processes have been allowed to continue

*Western azalea*

and because little disruption of the physical environment has occurred, plant life is varied and rich.

Taking the time to learn about Yosemite's wildflowers (and other plants) can be amazingly rewarding. Being able to identify and learn something about the various flowers and plants you encounter will enrich your park experience.

### Further Reading

*Discovering Sierra Trees* by Stephen F. Arno. Yosemite NP: Yosemite Association and Sequoia Natural History Association, 1973.

*An Illustrated Flora of Yosemite National Park* by Stephen J. Botti, illustrated by Walter Sydoriak. Yosemite NP: Yosemite Association, 2001.

*Sierra Nevada Tree Identifier* by Jim Paruk. Yosemite NP: Yosemite Association, 1997.

*Wildflowers of Yosemite* by Lynn and Jim Wilson and Jeff Nicholas. Yosemite NP: Sunrise Productions, 1987.

**Q:** What is the strange red plant (with no leaves or green of any kind) that is noticeable on the forest floor each spring?

**A:** Snow plant (*Sarcoides sanguinea*). A "saprophyte," it lives on decayed organic matter, appearing just after the snow melts each year.

*Snow plant*

*Spice bush*

## The Giant Sequoias

*A mature sequoia tree is 3,125,000,000,000,000,000,000 times larger than a single bacterium.*
—J. I. D. Hinds

After its granite cliffs and domes and its spectacular waterfalls, Yosemite is best known for its famous big trees, the giant sequoias. In fact, the 1864 Yosemite Grant set aside as a protected park only Yosemite Valley and the Mariposa Grove of Big Trees. These towering monarchs were recognized for their special qualities early in history, and they continue to inspire awe to this day.

The mature big trees can be recognized by their huge, columnar trunks that are free of branches for 100 to 150 feet. The foliage is blue-green and individual leaves create rounded sprays, unlike the flattened branchlets of the incense-cedar. The bark is quite fibrous, can be 4 to 24 inches thick, and is cinnamon-brown in color. This bark covering is non-resinous and very fire-resistant. Sequoia wood is pink when cut, then darkens to red. It is amazingly resistant to decay (many downed trees remain intact on the ground for years). Cones are quite small (2 or 3 inches), are abundant, and produce several hundred seeds each.

The giant sequoias *(Sequoiadendron giganteum)* grow from these tiny seeds that are no larger than flakes of oatmeal. You would have to amass over 90,000 seeds to produce a pound of them. Upon germination, a one-inch seedling results, and these seedlings grow into young trees through the years. These youngsters are characterized by a fairly symmetrical, cone-shaped appearance with sharply-pointed crowns.

Middle age is reached by sequoias when they are 700 or 800 years old. They are mature, have just about reached their maximum height, and have developed a rounded top. Some mature trees that have been burned are noted for their "snag tops." When fire damages the bases of the trees, water supply to their upper reaches is limited and the tops of the trees die. The trees remain healthy, but their appearance suggests the hazards and effects of age.

Scientists believe that the giant sequoia is the largest living thing in the world (though this is sometimes disputed). The trees stop growing upward at about 800 years of age, but they continue to add bulk. Maximum height seems to be about 320 feet, and diameters at the base vary depending on where the measurements are taken (there is quite a swelling at the base of each sequoia). Some trees at the base are over 35 feet in diameter, while at about 20 feet above the ground, that size drops to about 20 feet.

It is hard to grasp the enormity of the sequoias. One example that provides perspective is the largest branch on the Grizzly Giant tree in the Mariposa Grove. It is over 6 feet in diameter. At that size it is larger than the trunks of the largest specimens of most trees east of the Mississippi River. It is also larger than many of the conifers in Yosemite.

Despite their longevity, giant sequoias are not the oldest living things. That distinction is reserved for the bristlecone pines, which may live to be 5,000 years old. Sequoias are known to live at least 3,200 years, and John Muir reported finding an individual 4,000 years old.

Giant sequoias occur naturally only in the Sierra Nevada primarily at elevations between 5,000 and 7,000 feet. In Yosemite there are three big tree groves: the Mariposa Grove (see page 48), the Tuolumne Grove, and the Merced Grove (page 58). Any visit to Yosemite should include a trip to see these impressive trees.

### Further Reading

*The Sequoias of Yosemite National Park* by H. Thomas Harvey. Yosemite NP: Yosemite Association, 1978.

*A Guide to the Sequoia Groves of California* by Dwight Willard. Yosemite NP: Yosemite Association, 2000.

*The Enduring Giants* by Joseph H. Engbeck, Jr. Sacramento: California Dept. of Parks and Recreation, 1973.

*Sequoia cone and seeds*

*Sequoia seedling*

## Mammmals

Over 75 species of mammals have been recorded in Yosemite National Park. What follows are brief descriptions of some of those mammals, particularly those that are likely to be seen by visitors in the course of their stay in the park.

### Mule Deer

Having experienced a life free of threat from humans, the mule deer in Yosemite seem almost tame. You are likely to spot one or more of these graceful creatures anywhere in the park, but they are especially obvious in Yosemite Valley and in the Wawona meadow area.

Despite the fact that they seem unconcerned by humans, mule deer should be treated as any other wild animal. These deer should be given a wide berth and not be fed (nor should any other park animal); many injuries have been caused to visitors who have disturbed these animals in the course of offering them human food. Even deaths have resulted from gorings and from the blows delivered by the surprisingly sharp hooves of the mule deer. In fact, more injuries occur in Yosemite inflicted by deer each year than those caused by black bears or any other park animal.

The mule deer takes its name from its large, mule-like ears. Weighing up to 200 pounds, it is primarily a browse animal eating leaves and tender twigs from trees, grass, and other herbs. The male mule deer (the buck) grows antlers each year for use in the mating season or "rut" each fall. Despite popular belief, the age of a given buck cannot be determined by counting the number of antler points he sports.

Mule deer are very common in Yosemite and are seen chiefly between 3,500 and 8,500 feet. They stay below the snow line in winter, often dropping into the foothills that border the west side of the park. Common predators of the mule deer are the mountain lion and the coyote.

### Black Bear

The reaction of many people to the black bear is both fascination and fear. Because of the many stories that are told about bears throughout the national park system, there are plenty of misconceptions that exist about these largest of park mammals.

Yosemite's black bear is often confused with the grizzly bear, a species that no longer exists in the park. The grizzly once roamed the Sierra Nevada but was eliminated by hunters around the turn of the century. The last grizzly killing occurred in Yosemite in 1895, and the last authentic record of the killing of a grizzly in California was from 1922.

Grizzly bears are considerably more dangerous to humans than are black bears. Occasional black bear incidents do occur, but those mainly result from improper food storage by visitors. For information about storing your food properly see pages 17 & 85. Never feed the bears, and observe them at a distance (particularly when cubs are present)!

Despite their name, black bears can be brown, blonde, cinnamon, or black. There are no members of the brown bear species (or any other) in Yosemite. Individuals range in size from 250 to 500 pounds, although even bigger bears have been recorded.

These bears are omnivores – they will eat practically anything. Typical fare is insects, small rodents, berries, acorns, and seeds. But human food, from hot dogs to cookies, also appeals to park bears. Because dependence on a human-provided diet creates bears that become bold and are not afraid of people, the need to keep visitor food well-stored is even more acute.

Black bears can be observed throughout the park, particularly in the evenings. Many bears enter a den in winter for a period of sleep that is not true hibernation. Young are born in late winter and leave the den in spring to forage with their mother.

## Black Bears & Human Food

Each year black bears are killed in Yosemite National Park as a direct result of human carelessness and improper food storage.

Driven by their excellent sense of smell and enormous appetite, black bears are drawn to human food. Once they have had a taste of it, they continue to seek it out from any possible source, including backpacks, picnic tables, ice chests, and cars. In the course of pursuing this new food, their natural fear of humans fades, and some bears may become aggressive.

When bears become too aggressive, they often have to be killed. In 2000, there were 654 incidents involving bears, resulting in over $120,000 in damage; five bears had to be killed. The only way to prevent the continuing loss of bears is to make sure that all food and trash are stored properly.

## How to Store Food from Bears

"Food" includes any item with a scent, regardless of packaging. This includes items that you might not consider food such as canned goods, bottles, drinks, soaps, cosmetics, toiletries, perfumes, trash, empty ice chests, and unwashed food-preparation items.

## What If You See a Bear?

Never approach a bear, regardless of its size. If you encounter a bear in a developed area of the park or on a hiking trail, act immediately: yell, clap hands, bang pots together, or throw small stones or sticks toward the bear from a safe distance with the goal of scaring the bear (you don't want to injure it). If others are with you, stand together to present a more intimidating figure, but do not make the bear feel surrounded - you want the bear to run away!

Use caution if you see cubs, as a mother may act aggressively to defend them. Never try to retrieve anything once a bear has it. If you follow these recommendations and act immediately, you should be successful in scaring bears away. Report all bear encounters to a park ranger as soon as possible.

## Yosemite Wild Bear Project

A special group of "Keep Bears Wild" products, including t-shirts, enamel pins, and stuffed animal toys, have been developed for sale in Yosemite. Proceeds from the sales of these items directly benefit park bears through the Yosemite Wild Bear Project, a joint effort of the Yosemite Association, DNC Parks & Resorts at Yosemite, and the National Park Service. Among the many programs supported by the project is bear canister rentals for backpackers.

Donations are welcome to support the "Keep Bears Wild" effort (call 209 379-2646), and bear products can be seen and purchased online at www.yosemitestore.com.

| Location | Bear-Aware Food Storage |
|---|---|
| **Parking Areas** | Place food in food storage lockers if available, or in your hotel room or cabin (but not your tent cabin). Food must not be stored in vehicles after dark. Don't forget to clear vehicles of food wrappers, crumbs, and baby wipes. Food may be stored in vehicles during daylight hours only. |
| **Campgrounds** | All food must be stored in food storage lockers without exception, day and night. Each campsite contains a food storage locker (bear box) measuring 33" x 45" x 19". |
| **Tent Cabins** | All food must be stored in food storage lockers, day and night. In Curry Village, coin-operated lockers are available for small items. Never leave items with an odor in your tent. |
| **Hotel Rooms & Cabins** | All food must be kept inside your room or cabin. If you are not in your room, the windows and doors must be closed. |
| **Picnic Areas & On the Trail** | Do not leave food unattended. |
| **Backpacking** | Bear-resistant food canisters are strongly recommended and are required above 9,600 feet (see page 17). |

## Mountain Lion

Terror-inducing stories abound about these large members of the cat family, but while they are present in Yosemite, they are almost never seen and rarely interact with humans. Also know as the cougar, panther, or puma, the mountain lion preys on other mammals, primarily deer. Individuals are wary of people, and go out of their way to avoid contact with park visitors; they are not a serious threat to human safety.

Besides deer, the mountain lion also will eat a number of small mammals including marmots, rabbits, foxes, coyotes, and raccoons, and even porcupines and skunks when the pickings are slim. Because they help to keep Yosemite's deer population in check, mountain lions are considered an important component of the park ecosystem.

Mountain lions can weigh from 75 to 275 pounds, and are 6 to 9 feet long including the tail. They are recognized by their size, solid tannish-brown color, and extended tail. Females give birth to a litter of 1 to 6 cubs in the middle of every other summer. Moutain lions produce a number of cat-like sounds, including hisses, growls, and yowls, and the mating call has been likened to the screams of a hysterical woman.

## Humans and Mountain Lions

While mountain lion attacks on humans are extremely rare, they are possible. Generally, mountain lions are calm, quiet, and elusive. If you spot one, consider yourself privileged! The National Park Service offers the following safety recommendations:

- Do not leave pets or pet food outside and unattended, especially at dawn and dusk. Pets can attract mountain lions into developed areas.
- Avoid hiking alone. Watch children closely and never let them run ahead of you on the trail. Talk to children about mountain lions, and teach them what to do if they meet one (see below).
- Store food according to park regulations.

## What If You See a Mountain Lion?

- Never approach a mountain lion, especially if it is feeding or with kittens. Most mountain lions will try to avoid a confrontation. Always give them a way to escape.
- Don't run. Stay calm. Hold your ground, or back away slowly. Face the lion and stand upright. Do all you can to appear larger. Raise your arms. If you have small children with you, pick them up.
- If the lion behaves aggressively, wave your arms, shout, and throw objects at it. The goal is to convince it that your are not prey and may be dangerous yourself. If attacked, fight back!

## TRICKS FOR OBSERVING ANIMALS

Try strolling down a forest trail, or walk along the edge of a meadow. Avoid groups of people, as most animals are easily frightened. Consider the color of your clothing and don't wear white, it makes you too conspicuous. Darker shades are better. Walk slowly. When you see an animal, don't make quick movements. If you should come upon one, such as a deer or a squirrel, continue slowly so as not to alarm it. Stop to watch it when you are still some distance away. If you want to see an animal that has disappeared into a burrow – a marmot, ground squirrel or a mouse – find a comfortable place to sit and remain quiet. Usually it will reappear in a short time to see where you are and what you are doing. Watch for evidence of mammal activities, such as dens, trails in the grass, or piles of kitchen middens where squirrels have cut away the scales of pine cones. Watch, too, for holes dug where pine nuts or acorns have been buried. — from *Discovering Sierra Mammals*.

## Coyote

Normally a very shy mammal, the Yosemite coyote has become accustomed to the human presence and is commonly seen here, particularly in Yosemite Valley. In winter, these dog-like creatures often can be viewed hunting in snow-covered meadows.

The coyote is one mammal that makes its presence known by its call. There is nothing more haunting (some would contend frightening) than the late-night howling and barking of a group of coyotes.

Weighing 25 to 30 pounds, coyotes live on small animals (primarily rodents), although fawns and an occasional adult mule deer are taken. Coyotes can be identified by their long, grayish fur (which is lighter on the underside) and a darkish tail.

## Squirrels and Chipmunks

A variety of squirrels and chipmunks is present in Yosemite. Most visitors, particularly campers, will encounter one or more species of these active rodents.

The common squirrels are the California gray squirrel (all gray with a long bushy tail, often seen in trees), the Sierra chickaree (a reddish tree squirrel that chews on pine cones and squeaks a lot), Golden-mantled ground squirrel, and the California ground squirrel (a brown animal, speckled with white, which lives in burrows in the ground). At higher elevations, the common ground squirrel is the "picket pin" (or Belding ground squirrel), which seated in its erect posture looks like a stake driven into the ground.

There are at least 5 different species of chipmunks in the park. They are generally reddish- brown in color, smaller than the squirrels, and wear 4 light-colored stripes separated by dark on their backs. These chipmunks are remarkably animated and quick, and dig burrows in stumps or the ground that are very hard to find.

## Marmot

A common sight in the park's higher elevations is the yellow-bellied marmot; watch for these rotund fellows at Olmsted Point on the Tioga Road. Actually members of the squirrel family, marmots resemble woodchucks for which they are sometimes mistaken. They regularly sun themselves on subalpine rocks, and behave tamely at certain roadside turnouts. Please do not feed them.

The marmots are about 15 to 18 inches long and have an average weight of about 5 pounds. They are yellowish-brown, live in dens under rock piles or tree roots, and hibernate during the winter. Their shrill warning note is distinctive.

## Bighorn Sheep

Originally native to the Yosemite area, the Sierra Nevada bighorn sheep were eliminated here around 1900 as a result of hunting and the disease spread by domestic animals.

In 1986, a herd of bighorns was released in the Tioga Pass area of Yosemite in an effort by scientists and researchers to re-establish a viable population. To date the experiment has been a success. Additional transplants have augumented the herd, which has been able to reproduce and survive on its own.

Bighorn sheep are remarkable rock climbers able to ascend and descend amazingly steep terrain. Some sheep weigh up to 200 pounds and are 3 feet high at the shoulder. They are gray or buffy brown in color and grow hard, permanent horns. In the male, they spriral back sometimes into a full circle, while the females have small, slightly backward curving horns. Watch for these beautiful animals in the mountainous regions around Tioga Pass.

## Other Mammals

These brief descriptions have touched on but a few of the numerous mammals native to Yosemite. To learn more, consult the following books that will provide greater depth and detail.

## Further Reading

*Discovering Sierra Mammals* by Russell K. Grater. Yosemite NP: Yosemite Association and Sequoia Natural HistoryAssociation, 1978.

*Sierra Nevada Natural History* by Tracy I. Storer and Robert L. Usinger. Berkeley: University of California Press, 1963.

*Yellow-bellied marmot*

## Birds

**B**ecause Yosemite plays host to over 240 different kinds of birds, it is not practical to provide an exhaustive and detailed bird list here. As was the case with the mammals, the following are highlights of the species one is likely to encounter in the course of a visit.

### Steller's Jay

This is, undoubtedly, one bird that just about everybody notices in Yosemite. The jay is bright blue with a dark head and a very prominent crest. Unfazed by humans, it boldly alights on tables and other perches close to food, all the while screeching its disagreeable screech. Surprisingly, the Steller's jay also is capable of producing a soft, warbling song. When a group of jays encounters a hawk or owl, the raucous cacophony of shrieks and calls that goes up is almost overpowering.

### Acorn Woodpecker

In Yosemite Valley, the acorn woodpecker is the woodpecker you are likely to see. Colored black and white with a red head marking (sometimes there's yellow also), these industrious birds drill holes in trees,

telephone poles, and buildings and fill them with acorns that they eat later (along with the bugs that have entered the acorns). Their flight is a distinctive series of shallowly U-shaped glides, and they are exceptionally noisy, making a "wack-up, wack-up" call most often. Wherever you find oaks, you will find acorn woodpeckers.

### Western Tanager

Here is a bird that is hard to miss. Though not common, the tanager is brilliant yellow with a bright orangish-red head. Likely to be seen in Yosemite Valley in spring and summer, this gaudy bird will sometimes

come to your picnic table or the ground near you. This may be the only bird in Yosemite with "day-glo" feathers.

### Belted Kingfisher

Along the Merced River and other bodies of water in the park, this striking blue bird can be seen flying low or perched on branches and snags, watching for fish and aquatic insects. If you're lucky, one will plunge into the water and emerge with dinner in its beak. There is a noticeable crest and a reddish band on the chest. You'll know its a kingfisher if you hear a loud rattling, clicking call.

### American Dipper

Another water bird, the dipper is truly phenomenal. Though gray and non-descript, these acrobatic creatures are named for their habit of bobbing up and down almost constantly. What's so phenomenal about them is their ability to fly into a stream or river and walk upstream underwater along the bottom clinging to rocks as they search for food. As you stroll beside a stream or river, keep a close eye for the amazing dipper!

### Clark's Nutcracker

The high country counterpart of the Steller's jay is the Clark's nutcracker. Also known as the "camp robber," this white, gray, and black bird with a prominent beak has a harsh, cawing voice. Very conspicuous in areas around Tuolumne Meadows, the Clark's nutcracker does crack and eat pine nuts, but is not averse to cleaning up around your campsite. You'll see these birds typically above 9,000 feet.

American dipper

## Black-headed Grosbeak

While picnicking or camping, you may see this other common Yosemite Valley resident. The grosbeak is characterized by its black, white, and orange markings and by its "gross beak" that is used for opening seeds. Oftentimes woods echo with the grosbeak's delightfully lyrical song that has been called a rich warble. The black-headed grosbeak is a sure sign of spring.

## Great Horned Owl

You may never get a glimpse of this bird, but chances are good you may hear one. This nocturnal dweller of most of the park's life zones is active from dusk until dawn. Most of that time it issues a series of deep, sonorous hoots. If you happen to hear the horned owl, see if you can locate its perch. These owls are excellent ventriloquists, so don't be surprised if you fail. Large ear tufts are sure signs that you're looking at the great horned owl.

## Other Birds

There's a whole lot to be learned about Yosemite's birds, and plenty of ways to learn it. Try a ranger-led bird walk, or pick up a pair of binoculars and see what there is to see. The books listed are great guides and will make your bird education easier for you.

## Yosemite's Ten "Most Wanted" Birds

Serious, sometimes fanatic, birdwatchers (or "birders") often keep a list of every bird known to occur in North America; its known as their personal "life list." When they see a bird they've never seen before, they will check it off the list. The goal is to see every single species on the list. There are several birds in Yosemite that are rarely seen anywhere else. These "most wanted" birds are feverishly sought by many zealous birdwatchers for their life lists.

1. Gray-crowned Rosy-finch
2. Great Gray Owl
3. Peregrine Falcon
4. Black-Backed Woodpecker
5. Flammulated Owl
6. Northern Goshawk
7. Pileated Woodpecker
8. Williamson's Sapsucker
9. Northern Pygmy Owl
10. Black Swift

Great horned owl          Great gray owl

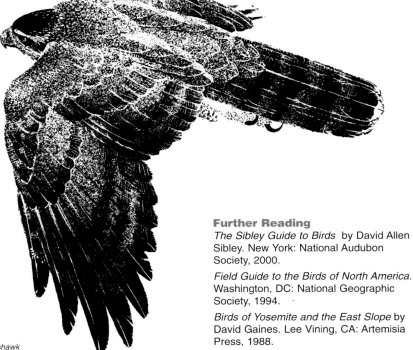

*Goshawk*

## Further Reading

*The Sibley Guide to Birds* by David Allen Sibley. New York: National Audubon Society, 2000.

*Field Guide to the Birds of North America.* Washington, DC: National Geographic Society, 1994.

*Birds of Yosemite and the East Slope* by David Gaines. Lee Vining, CA: Artemisia Press, 1988.

## Reptiles & Amphibians

*L*izards, frogs, and snakes are all members of this group of Yosemite wildlife. About 40 different species of amphibians and reptiles are known to have established populations in the Yosemite Sierra, and there are no doubt more.

All of the lizards in Yosemite are harmless reptiles. Because they prefer warm locations, they are found primarily in the lower elevations of the park (Yosemite Valley and below). Most commonly seen is the western fence lizard. He's black or blotched brownish-gray on top with a blue throat and belly.

At least 14 different types of snakes inhabit the park. With the exception of the western rattlesnake, they are all non-poisonous. The most regularly-seen species is the garter snake, which frequents meadows, ponds, streams, and lakes (it's a remarkably good swimmer). The garter snake is black, gray, or dark brown with a cream-colored strip down its back and usually red blotches on its sides.

The western rattlesnake is Yosemite's only venomous snake, but rarely bites people. The rattler varies from cream to black in color with a variety of blotches. The head is broad, flat, and triangular, and when surprised, the snake will coil and shake the rattles it sports at the end of its tail. The result is a buzzing sound that is a warning to stay away.

Frogs and toads are abundant in Yosemite; there are a minimum of 8 different kinds. You are more likely to hear from these denizens of the park than to see them. Most abundant is the Pacific tree frog, a small, green, gray, or brown fellow with a black mask and a constantly-heard year-round song. Recently it has been determined that the mountain yellow-

*Pacific tree frog*

legged frog, quite common 20 to 30 years ago, is in steep decline and possibly disappearing from the park.

The last of the amphibians are the salamanders and newts. These small, slimy creatures like it moist and dark. That's why they're rarely seen. Most likely to be discovered is the California newt, the brownish-orange newt that is often spotted after a heavy rain. Two species of salamander are found almost nowhere else but in the Yosemite region: the Mt. Lyell and the limestone salamanders.

### Further Reading

*Discovering Sierra Reptiles and Amphibians* by Harold Basey. Yosemite NP: Yosemite Association and Sequoia Natural History Association, 1976.

*California Amphibians and Reptiles* by Robert C. Stebbins. Berkeley: University of California Press, 1972.

**Q:** Can rattlesnakes swim?

**A:** Yes, quite well. Their long right lungs provide increased buoyancy. They usually hold their rattles high and dry and may strike while in water.

*Western rattlesnake*

## Fishes

**D**espite the impression of many people that the Yosemite region is dotted with lakes and streams laden with native trout, there is only one game fish that naturally occurs in the park. That's the rainbow trout. There are five other native species, but they are relatively uncommon and are not game fishes (the Sacramento sucker, the Sacramento squawfish, the hardhead, the California roach, and the riffle sculpin).

When the glaciers moved through Yosemite during the last ice age, native fish populations were eliminated and most of the park's lakes and streams were left fish-less. One job of the U.S. Army in Yosemite National Park between 1890 and 1914 was to plant new fish species in the high country and provide greater opportunities for sport fisher-people. Non-native species that were introduced and now occur in the park are the cutthroat trout, the golden trout, the brown trout, and the brook trout. The brook and brown trout have adapted best.

For information about fishing in Yosemite, see page 29. For additional, more in-depth coverage of the park's fish family, see the sources at right.

*Riffle sculpin*

**Q:** What is the oldest record of trout planting in Yosemite Valley?

**A:** April 1, 1879, when the Yosemite Fish Commission began planting 20,000 young trout in the different streams of the valley.

## A List of the Fishes of Yosemite National Park
("N" denotes a native species)

### Trout
Brook trout *(Salvelinus fontinalis)*
Brown trout *(Salmo trutta)*
Cutthroat trout *(Salmo clarkii)*
Golden trout *(Salmo aguabonita)*
Rainbow trout *(Salmo gairdnerii)* N

### Suckers
Sacramento sucker *(Catostomus occidentalis)* N

*Mouth of Sacramento sucker*

### Minnows
California roach *(Hesperoleucus symmetricus)* N
Hardhead *(Mylopharodon conocephalus)* N
Sacramento squawfish *(Ptychocheilus grandis)* N

### Sculpins
Riffle sculpin *(Cottus gulosus)* N

### Further Reading
*Fishes of Yosemite National Park* by Willis A. Evans, Orthello Wallis, and Glenn D. Gallison. Yosemite NP: Yosemite Natural History Association, 1961. (Out of print).

*Yosemite Trout Fishing* by Hank Johnston. Yosemite NP: Flying Spur Press, 1985.

*Sierra Trout Guide* by Ralph Cutter. Portland: Frank Amato Publications, 1984.

*Ranger plants fish in Yosemite lake, a practice now discontinued*

## The Poisonous, The Itchy & The Sickening

The relatively undeveloped landscape of Yosemite Valley and the vast regions of wilderness around it are home to plants, animals, and other organisms that may in one way or another be hazardous to your health. The threat from these sources is generally not serious, and there are a number of precautions you can take and signs to watch for to avoid problems. Whatever you do, don't become frightened by the following list.

### Rattlesnakes

These wriggly reptiles are the only poisonous snakes in Yosemite. Out hiking, you will rarely encounter a rattler, and if you do it will almost always buzz its rattles when threatened. If you happen upon a rattlesnake, keep a safe distance and leave. Do not try to kill it or scare it away. It's always a good idea to watch carefully where you walk, where you put your hands, and where you sit.

### Scorpions

In Yosemite's lower elevations, this threatening-looking insect hides by day and becomes active at night. The sting delivered by the scorpion is painful but not at all dangerous to humans. Scorpions hide under rocks and logs, so be cautious when you're lifting or rolling such objects.

### Giardia Lamblia

This funny sounding creature is a protozoan that causes an intestinal disease called giardiasis. Its symptoms are chronic diarrhea, abdominal cramps, bloating, fatigue, and weight loss. Because giardia has been found to be present in park lakes and streams, you should purify any drinking water that is not from the tap. Either boil it for three minutes, use an iodine-based purifier, or use a giardia-rated water filter.

### Mosquitos

These delightful insects have been characterized by one writer as the "most bothersome of the animal life in the High Sierra." Though relatively benign individually, roving bands of mosquitos can make the lives of visitors, particularly in certain areas of the wilderness, totally miserable. They breed in locations with standing water, so they are common wherever there is snow melt. Typically, that means 4,000 feet at the end of May advancing upwards to 10,000 feet by late July. What can be done about these pesky pests? Try repellents, long pants and long-sleeved shirts, and mosquito-net hats and tents. If you're backpacking, locate your camp to take advantge of any breeze and away from areas of moisture.

### Ticks

Some park ticks, the small bugs that suck blood from a variety of mammals, carry an illness known as Lyme disease. Not every tick, however, is a carrier. Symptoms of the disease in its advanced form can include arthritis, meningitis, neurological problems, and cardiac symptoms, and the disease can be very serious. If it is detected early, treatment can cure or lessen the severity of the disease. If you think you might have been bitten by a tick, watch for a rash at the spot of the bite and for symptoms of the flu. If you contract Lyme disease and you believe its source was Yosemite, please call the Park Sanitarian at (209) 379-1033.

*Poison oak*

### Poison Oak

This is one of the most widespread shrubs in California, and it's quite abundant in Yosemite's lower reaches. Fluids from the plant produce an irritating rash on the skin of humans and it can sometimes be very severe. Sufferers itch terrifically and can experience swelling. If you think you've been in poison oak, wash your body and clothes thoroughly to remove the oily fluid.

### Spiders

There are a couple of interesting critters in this category. The single truly dangerous spider in Yosemite is the black widow. With its black, orb-shaped body featuring a red "hour glass" pattern on its underside, this arachnid is easy to identify. The black widow is not aggressive, but when disturbed can bite and inject a nerve poison that can cause severe symptoms and even death. If bitten, see a physician quickly. Much more fearsome in appearance is the tarantula, but this big, woolly fellow is fairly benign. Up to four inches across, tarantulas are active at night and don't bite unless provoked. The bite is painful but not dangerous.

## Yosemite's Endangered Species

While Yosemite National Park is abundant with varied plant and animal life, several indigenous species have been lost to extinction over the years, and threats to park life forms persist despite the National Park Service's best efforts to protect them. Grizzly bears were once residents of the Yosemite Sierra, and other birds, mammals, and plants have been lost.

Some species of plants and animals, though still present, have undergone local, state, or national declines, raising concerns about their possible extinction if protective measures are not implemented. As a result, the U.S. Fish and Wildlife Service, California Department of Fish and Game, and Yosemite National Park have established categories for these species that reflect the urgency of their status, and the need for monitoring, protection, and implementation of recovery actions.

Not all threats to park wildlife are controllable at Yosemite. Take the peregrine falcon. These impressive flyers eat birds that migrate to Central and South America each winter. Use of pesticides is much more common in these wintering areas, and DDT has found its way into the systems of many Yosemite peregrines. The result is that the eggs they lay became thin-shelled and subject to breakage. Nesting success dropped dramatically, and park officials feared that peregrines might be lost for good.

But through a fairly complicated augmentation procedure, the National Park Service has seen a growth in peregrine numbers and nests. During the nesting season, climbers were employed to reach peregrine nests and remove the fragile eggs. They were replaced with plastic phonies. Captive-raised chicks were later placed in the nests, and the parents adopted the newcomers without hesitation. Work continues to encourage other countries to limit their use of harmful chemicals.

Other significant programs have involved the restoration of meadows, oak woodlands, and other park areas. As well, a number of revegetation efforts are underway to reclaim portions of Yosemite that have been over-used and stripped of any plant life. Watch for evidence of this important work as you travel throughout the park, and be sure your use of Yosemite is consistent with the protection of the plants and animals here.

### Yosemite Species Listed as At Risk by the U.S. Government

**Endangered**
Sierra Nevada bighorn sheep

**Threatened**
Bald eagle
Red-legged frog
Valley elderberry longhorn beetle

**Plant Species of Concern**
Bolander's clover
Congdon's lomatium
Slender-stemmed monkeyflower
Three-bracted onion
Tiehm's rock-cress
Yosemite woolly sunflower

### Yosemite Species Listed as At Risk by the State of California

**Endangered**
Bald eagle
Great gray owl
Peregrine falcon
Willow flycatcher

**Threatened**
California wolverine
Limestone salamander
Sierra Nevada red fox

**Rare Plant Species**
Congdon's lewisia
Congdon's woolly-sunflower
Tompkin's sedge
Yosemite onion

Source: Final Yosemite Valley Plan/Supplemental EIS

*Bighorn sheep*

# Yosemite's History

*U.S. Cavalry in Yosemite Valley, circa 1906*

The recorded history of Yosemite National Park is as fascinating and important as it is short relative to that of other parts of our country and the world. While Native Americans were long-term residents, Yosemite Valley was not entered by European Americans until 1851, and not really occupied by them in any meaningful way until the last quarter of the nineteenth century.

These historical events are particularly significant because the actions of both men and governments in and relating to Yosemite proved to be pioneering efforts in the conservation of natural areas all around the globe. There is little question that at Yosemite the concept of national parks was born, and the park still serves as a model and symbol for the entire world.

## Yosemite's Native People

Indians resided in the Yosemite region for about 4,000 years before the Spaniards occupied California and the Gold Rush occurred. Anthropologists suggest that the earliest Indian inhabitants came from the east side of the Sierra Nevada looking for water and food in particularly dry years. Later, groups from the Central Valley (predominantly Miwok-speaking) invaded the foothills and greater Yosemite as Indian populations increased and competition for homeland grew. The Miwoks and the people from the east side came together and established permanent villages near the Merced River throughout Yosemite Valley.

Obviously, there is no recorded history of the Yosemite Miwoks until very recent times. Anthropologists believe that the Miwok culture evolved very slowly. Their simple lifestyle remained relatively unchanged, no doubt, for centuries. The Yosemites' basically primitive existence involved seed and plant gathering, hunting, and trading. Generally, they spent fall and winter in Yosemite Valley or the warmer foothills, then roamed into Yosemite's high country in spring and summer in quest of game and to barter with Mono Lake Paiutes and other people from east of the area.

*Miwok bow*

Indian people in California were brought in contact with Euro-Americans with the advent of the Spanish missions in the late 18th century. As the central and southern parts of the state became settled, white encroachment on traditional Indian territory increased. There is no evidence of this fact, but some believe that at the beginning of the 1800s the Indian people of Yosemite were struck with a "fatal black sickness," a plague of some type. Reportedly, the few survivors abandoned the valley and relocated to the eastern Sierra and were assimilated by other groups there. For a number of years (the exact number unknown), Yosemite Valley may have been uninhabited.

One of the offspring of the Yosemite people who grew up with the Mono Paiutes was Tenaya (see page 107). As a youth, Tenaya had heard stories of the beauty and bounty of Yosemite Valley. He finally visited the former home of his people quite late in his life. Being favorably impressed, he and 200 other Indians (some Yosemite Miwoks, some not) resettled the valley. Tenaya was named chief of the group.

These Indians lived in relative harmony in the valley they called "Ah-wah-nee" until the fateful Euro-American occupation of the Sierra foothills around 1850. Ahwahnee (as it is spelled now) probably means "place of a gaping mouth," although Lafayette Bunnell of the Mariposa Battalion reported that through hand signals the native people had indicated its meaning was "deep, grassy valley."

As friction between gold seekers and foothill Indians increased, anti-Indian sentiments blossomed. Groups from the Central Valley moved higher into the foothills, and conflict resulted both between Indians and whites and between rival Indian groups. As Tenaya and his fellows defiantly protected their mountain stronghold, violence did occur. The Mariposa Battalion was formed to locate, capture, and relocate to reservations the native residents, and the story of its discovery of Yosemite Valley and its removal of the Indian people is well known.

The white soldiers called the Indians the "Yosemites," from the Miwok word "uzumati" or grizzly bear. (The natives called themselves the Ahwahneechees.) Some consider this a corruption of the Ahwahneechee word "Yo-che-ma-te" which means "some among them are killers." Whatever the true meaning, the local Indians were known as fierce fighters who lived in an area where grizzly bears were fairly common.

Following Tenaya's death in 1853, what was left of the band of Yosemite Indians dispersed to other locations. Some went east to the Mono Lake area, while others joined neighboring peoples along the Tuolumne River. Never again did the remaining Yosemites gather together as a people.

Within twenty years, the number of native Indians living in the Yosemite area dwindled to below fifty. With white settlement of Yosemite Valley and ever increasing visita-

*Obsidian arrow points*

tion, the native Miwok culture was irrevocably corrupted.

Hotelkeepers and other concessioners employed some of the Indians for odd jobs and manual labor, but the Yosemites were only tolerated at best.

## A Gentle Lifestyle

During their hundreds of years of occupation of Yosemite Valley, the Yosemite Miwoks were remarkably gentle in their use of the land. There were at least forty different camp spots on the floor of the valley. Most of them were summer encampments only. Because of heavy snow and extremely cold temperatures, the bulk of the valley residents moved to the El Portal area and the foothills below to pass the severe winter months.

The houses of the people were rude structures covered primarily by slabs of cedar bark. The typical house was a conical lean-to sporting three layers of bark and affording reasonable shelter from the elements. The Yosemite Miwoks also built earth-covered dance and sweat houses, and small elevated granaries for storing acorns and other edibles.

Native foodstuffs were hunted and gathered (very little cultivation was done).The staple of the Indian diet was acorn, which was elaborately prepared and eaten as mush. Other vegetation such as mushrooms, ferns, clover, and bulbs was also eaten. Fish and game included deer, squirrels, rabbits, rainbow trout, and the Sacramento sucker. Some insects like certain fly larvae, caterpillars, and grasshop-

*Miwok basket*

pers were considered delicacies.

Products of the Yosemite Indian culture included fairly coarse twined baskets and more fine-coiled baskets with elaborate patterns, as well as cradles, bows and arrows, obsidian tools and implements, bone awls and scrapers, and some ceremonial costumes.

Today the only noticeable evidence of the habitation of Yosemite Valley by native peoples is the occasional discovery of an obsidian flake or a granite grinding hole.

**Q:** What is the shiny black substance used by the Indians for making arrowheads and other implements?

**A:** Obsidian, a volcanic glass common on the east side of the Sierra Nevada. The Yosemites would trade acorns and other items with their eastern neighbors for obsidian.

*Chief Lemee dressed for traditional Miwok dance*

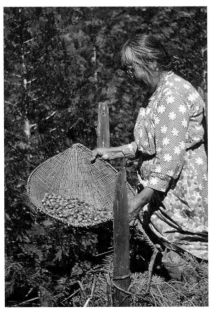

*Maggie Howard places acorns in storage chuk-ah*

## The Euro-American Occupation

Yosemite Valley was sighted by Euro-Americans for the first time in 1833. A party of explorers headed by Joseph Rutherford Walker was crossing the Sierra Nevada that fall, and in their efforts to determine the best route, several of the group came upon the north rim of the valley. The cliffs were described as "more than a mile high," and after several efforts the mountaineers determined that they were "utterly impossible for a man to descend, to say nothing of our horses."

Some twenty years later, the valley was finally entered by someone other than Native Americans.

In response to actions by the Yosemite Indians and their neighbors in defense of their homeland, a group of men was organized as the Mariposa Battalion to kill Indians as necessary and to transport survivors to reservations in the Central Valley. A punitive expedition was mounted in March of 1851, and their quest for Indians led the battalion into Yosemite Valley, where they beheld what no other group of pioneers had seen before.

*Yosemite Falls by artist Thomas Ayres, 1855*

It wasn't long before the word began to spread about Yosemite's wonders. Letters from members of the Mariposa Battalion to San Francisco newspapers aroused the interest of James Mason Hutchings, who organized the first tourist party to Yosemite Valley in 1855. He brought the artist, Thomas Ayres, who made sketches of the geologic features, which sketches Hutchings used to disseminate Yosemite's fame even more widely.

An increasing stream of visitors arrived primarily on foot and horseback, but as the years passed, wagon roads were developed to permit yet greater visitation.

Hutchings became the chief entrepreneur and publicist for Yosemite, homesteading land and operating a hotel for early tourists. Other hotels and residences were built, livestock was grazed in the meadows, crops were planted, orchards were established, and Yosemite Valley was treated as no more than a resource to be exploited.

*Clark's Station, circa 1860*

### The State Grant

Fortunately, not everyone viewed the valley as a capitalist's dream come true. Some amazingly farsighted persons took it upon themselves to work for the protection of Yosemite Valley for the public good. These early day conservationists, I. W. Raymond and Frederick Law Olmsted (the landscape architect who later designed New York's Central Park) prominent among them, appealed to Congress. Senator John Conness introduced a bill to grant Yosemite Valley and the Mariposa Grove of Big Trees to the State of California for preservation and protection. The bill was passed, and President Abraham Lincoln interrupted his preoccupation with the Civil War to sign the legislation on June 30, 1864.

It was a landmark event. Never before had a government set aside a piece of land for its inherent natural and scenic qualities to be preserved for the public use, resort and recreation "inalienable for all time." Yosemite became, in effect, the first state park and the first national park in the world. It unquestionably served as a model for the development of other parks and led to the birth of the U.S. National Park System as we know it today.

### Public Management

Responsibility for management of the Yosemite Grant (as it came to be called) fell to a Board of Commissioners appointed by California's governor and to the "Guardian" that the board hired. Yosemite's first Guardian was Galen Clark (see page 107).

The 1860s and '70s saw improved access to the valley thanks to the completion of several wagon roads, and the Guardian

*Cooke's Hotel, mid 1880s*

had to contend with an astounding rise in visitation.

Many new hostelries were built including the extravagant Cosmopolitan Saloon and Bathhouse, Black's Hotel, Leidig's Hotel, La Casa Nevada Hotel, the Stoneman House, and others. Competition was fierce among the various operators, and unsuspecting visitors found themselves heavily lobbied by concessioners seeking their business.

Things in Yosemite were far from peaceful and quiet, however. Given the intense public interest in Yosemite as well as the disappointment of the original homesteaders who saw their opportunities to make a killing disappear, Yosemite politics were never boring. Several lawsuits were brought by individuals who were dispossessed by the Yosemite Grant (Hutchings foremost among them), and criticism was regularly leveled at the Board of Commissioners for its alleged poor management.

### Greater Yosemite

While Yosemite Valley and the Big Trees had been recognized and protected, the thousands of acres of wilderness surrounding these relatively small park strongholds had not. Led by John Muir (see page 108) and by Easterner Robert Underwood Johnson (editor of the then influential *Century Magazine*), a group of preservationists began to focus attention on the need to protect the greater Yosemite area including the beautiful high country regions like Tuolumne Meadows.

As resource degradation in the form of mining, logging, and stock grazing increased, so did the efforts of Yosemite champions. Muir and Johnson did their

best to influence Congress and to inform the American people about the threats to the Yosemite. They derived important support from the Southern Pacific Railroad and its president, Edward Harriman, who were strongly interested in boosting tourism in the Sierra Nevada.

On October 1, 1890, the U.S. government acknowledged the preciousness of these wildlands by enacting the law that established Yosemite National Park. Interestingly, Yosemite National Park did not include Yosemite Valley or the Mariposa Grove, but encompassed an enormous area around them. The park was actually 30% larger than it is today.

*Early visitors pose before Yosemite Falls*

## The Army Takes Control

*T*he brand new national park needed management, and in 1890, the National Park Service had not yet been established. It was determined that the U.S. Army would assume the administration of Yosemite (as they had at other national parks), and members of the cavalry became a common sight in the park. Because much of the area was covered by a deep blanket of snow during the winter months, the Army limited its occupation of Yosemite to summers only. Usually soldiers from San Francisco would ride or march to and from their headquarters in Wawona each summer.

The duties of the cavalrymen were multiple and varied. They chased sheepherders from high country meadows, explored previously uncharted regions of the park blazing trails and preparing maps, surveyed boundaries, and prevented poachers from illegally taking park game. The work done by Army personnel was prodigious, and their mark on Yosemite's history was a major one.

During the Spanish-American War, when many U.S. troops were engaged, civilian rangers were hired by the Army to assist at the park. They were the first of their kind.

The existence of two different administrations, one for Yosemite Valley and the Mariposa Grove of Big Trees, the other for the greater Yosemite National Park, inevitably led to duplication, overlap, and conflict. Many individuals and organizations (including John Muir and the Sierra Club) began to push for a unification of all of Yosemite under the management of one entity.

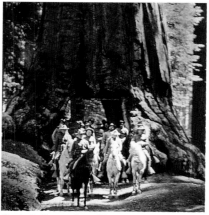

*Cavalry in Wawona Tunnel Tree*

### A Single Yosemite

The mood of the public was apparently shared by lawmakers and government officials. In 1906, the federal government formally accepted the "recession" of Yosemite Valley and the Mariposa Grove from the State of California, an action that obviated the Yosemite Grant once and for all. The price of the agreement was the reduction in overall size of the park to conform it to natural boundaries and to exclude private mining and timber holdings. But at last there was one Yosemite National Park with a single administration.

The U.S. Army continued its management of the park, moving its headquarters to Yosemite Valley (to a site near the present-day Yosemite Lodge). In 1914, a civilian administration was established, and the first "park rangers" were authorized and employed by the Department of the Interior.

### The Army Years

The years between 1890 and 1914 were characterized by a transportation revolution. Regular stage lines began operation, and private wagons commonly made the trip to Yosemite. Visitation continued its remarkable expansion, and the completion of the Yosemite Valley Railroad from Merced to El Portal in 1907 effectively heralded the end of the stagecoach era in Yosemite. But more earthshaking changes in transportation were still to come.

In 1900, the first automobile entered Yosemite Valley (albeit illegally). The U.S. Army officially allowed automobiles into the park in 1913, and when they came, they came with a vengeance. Two years later, all horse-drawn stages connecting train passengers to Yosemite Valley were replaced by motor stages. By 1920, two-thirds of all visitors were coming to Yosemite via private automobile.

The period also witnessed growth and proliferation of concessioner facilities. Public campgrounds were initiated, Camp Curry was established, Best's Studio was founded, and Camp Ahwahnee was built at the base of Sentinel Rock. Competition remained hot and heavy, and considerable conflict resulted between concessioners.

A regrettable chapter in Yosemite's history was written during the Army years. The famous and bitter battle over the damming of the Hetch Hetchy Valley was settled in 1913 with the enactment of the Raker Act, and the resulting inundation of the area. See page 57 for more about the Hetch Hetchy controversy.

**Q:** Who was the first permanent Euro-American resident of Yosemite Valley?

**A:** James Lamon who took up a preemption claim in the Valley's east end in 1859 and built a cabin. Apple trees he planted still grow near Curry Village and the stables.

## The National Park Service

A major change came about in the National Park System with the creation of the National Park Service in 1916. It had been recognized that administration of the parks required more than the part-time attention of the Army and that there was a war to be fought in Europe. The National Park Service was the Interior Department's chosen alternative.

It was Frederick Law Olmsted, Jr. (whose father had been influential in the establishment of the 1864 Yosemite Grant), who proposed that the purpose of the new agency should be "to conserve the scenery and the natural and historic objects and the wildlife therein, and to provide for the enjoyment of the same in such manner and by such means as will leave them unimpaired for the enjoyment of future generations." This phrase became the cornerstone of the act that created the N.P.S. and guides the agency still.

The years following 1916 were significant not only for Yosemite but also for all U.S. national parks because the basic policies of the agency were being developed and implemented. The process of interpreting the N.P.S. mandate to preserve the parks while allowing for their use was ongoing. Yosemite consistently was the park where new ideas were first tested and applied.

Yosemite's new National Park Service Superintendent was Washington B. "Dusty" Lewis, who was responsible for many innovations and changes at the park. During his twelve-year tenure the concessions were consolidated under one principal operating company (The Yosemite Park & Curry Company), roads including the Tioga Road were improved and tolls eliminated, new accommodations were built in Yosemite Valley (Yosemite Lodge and the Ahwahnee Hotel) and at Glacier Point, a new administrative center was constructed, and modernization of utilities, roads, and buildings was accomplished.

### Interpretation

It was also shortly after the birth of the park service that Yosemite personnel inaugurated the educational program so familiar to park visitors today. Known as "interpretation," the original program was the inspiration of Dr. C. M. Goethe, and Harold Bryant and Loye Miller were hired as Yosemite's first "nature guides" in 1920. At the outset the interpretive program was pretty much limited to nature walks, but it has evolved to include visitor center displays, campfire programs, informal talks, multi-media presentations, and informational literature.

A logical extension of the interpretive program was the Yosemite Museum, plans for which were hatched about 1921. Several years later a permanent museum was completed in the park thanks to a gift from the Laura Spelman Rockefeller Memorial. At the same time a Field School of Natural History was established in Yosemite to provide for the training of future interpreters and nature guides.

These formative years of the N.P.S. reflected the realization that protection of the parks depended on a strong program of education designed to increase public awareness of the special values embodied by Yosemite and other outstanding natural areas. The Yosemite model has been emulated throughout the world and is still as vital as it was eighty years ago.

### The Modern Years

The past seventy-five years in Yosemite have seen consistent management and burgeoning visitation. With scientific research and experience, resource policies have changed. Fire is no longer viewed as evil, wild animals are managed to be wild, and artificial attractions like the Fire Fall from Glacier Point have been eliminated.

The greatest challenge facing Yosemite today is its popularity. With visitation hovering around four million each year, the park sometimes suffers from overcrowding, congestion, and air pollution. Effects of these conditions are often resource degradation and a diminished experience for visitors. It can only be hoped that the coming years will provide solutions to these thorny problems and that Yosemite will long remain the preeminent national park in the world.

### Further Reading

*Discovery of the Yosemite* by Lafayette H. Bunnell. First published in 1911. Yosemite NP: Yosemite Association, 1990.

*One Hundred Years in Yosemite* by Carl P. Russell. Omnibus edition. Yosemite NP: Yosemite Association, 1992.

*The Yosemite Grant, 1864-1906: A Pictorial History* by Hank Johnston. Yosemite NP: Yosemite Association, 1995

*Yosemite Indians* by Elizabeth Godfrey. Revised edition. Yosemite NP: Yosemite Association, 1977.

## A Yosemite Chronology

**1833**—Yosemite Valley was first seen by Euro-Americans. The Joseph Walker party in crossing the Sierra encountered a valley with "precipices more than a mile high" that were "impossible for a man to descend."

**1851**—The Mariposa Battalion under the command of Major James Savage became the first group of pioneers to enter Yosemite Valley. They were pursuing "intransigent" Indians.

**1852**—The Mariposa Grove of Big Trees was discovered by a party of prospectors.

**1855**—The first tourist party visited Yosemite Valley with James Mason Hutchings as guide. Thomas Ayres, an artist with the group, made the first known sketches of Yosemite Valley.

**1856**—The first permanent structure, The Lower Hotel, was built in Yosemite Valley at the base of Sentinel Rock. The first trail into Yosemite Valley was completed by Milton and Houston Mann.

**1859**—The first photograph in Yosemite Valley was made by C. L. Weed. His subject was the Upper Hotel.

**1864**—Yosemite Valley and the Mariposa Grove of Big Trees were set aside by the federal government as the first state park in the world. Florence Hutchings was the first white child to be born in Yosemite Valley.

*Cavalry in Mariposa Grove of Big Trees, circa 1890*

**1866**—Galen Clark was named the first Yosemite Guardian.

**1868**—John Muir made his first trip to Yosemite.

**1871**—The first ascent of Mt. Lyell, Yosemite's highest peak, was accomplished by J. B. Tileston on August 29.

**1874**—The first road into Yosemite Valley, the Coulterville Road, was completed. The Big Oak Flat Road was finished a month later.

**1875**—George Anderson made the first ascent of Half Dome before the installation of ropes or cables. The first public school was opened in Yosemite Valley.

**1876**—John Muir's first article on the devastation of meadows in the Sierra Nevada by sheep was published.

**1878**—The first public campgrounds were opened in Yosemite Valley by A. Harris near the site of the present-day Ahwahnee Hotel.

*Early campers in Yosemite Valley*

**1890**—Yosemite National Park established. The park did not include Yosemite Valley or the Mariposa Big Trees, but encompassed a large region around them.

**1891**—The first telephones were installed in Yosemite Valley.

**1892**—Trout were first planted in Yosemite waters by the California Fish and Game Commission.

**1896**—Firearms were prohibited from the park.

**1898**—The first civilian park ranger, Archie Leonard, was employed at Yosemite.

**1900**—The first automobile (a Locomobile) was driven into Yosemite by Oliver Lippincott and Edward C. Russell.

**1907**—The first railway line to Yosemite, the Yosemite Valley Railroad, began operation.

**1913**—Automobiles were "officially" admitted to Yosemite.

**1915**—First appropriation for the construction of the John Muir Trail approved.

**1916**—The National Park Service was established. Washington B. Lewis was named the first N.P.S. Superintendent at Yosemite.

**1917**—The first High Sierra Camp, Tuolumne Meadows Lodge, was installed.

**1919**—The first airplane, piloted by Lt. J. S. Krull, landed in Yosemite Valley on May 27.

**1921**—The first installations in the Yosemite Museum were completed.

**1926**—The Yosemite Museum opened to the public.

**1934**—The first water from the Hetch Hetchy Reservoir flowed into San Francisco.

**1935**—Badger Pass Ski Area was developed.

**1940**—Ostrander Ski Hut was opened for winter use.

**1946**—The first ascent of the Lost Arrow Spire by four climbers was accomplished on September 2.

**1949**—The first use of a helicopter for rescue purposes was made at Benson Lake to fly an injured boy to safety.

**1951**—The first airplane planting of trout was done in Yosemite.

**1954**—Park visitation exceeded the one million level for the first time in history; 1,008,031 visitors were recorded.

**1958**—The first climb up the face of El Capitan was completed.

**1961**—Pioneer Yosemite History Center opened to the public.

**1966**—New Yosemite Valley Visitor Center built.

**1967**—For the first time over 2 million visitors were recorded.

**1969**—The "fire fall" from Glacier Point was discontinued. The famed "Wawona Tunnel Tree" toppled over from the weight of its winter snow load.

**1970**—The free shuttle bus system was initiated in Yosemite Valley.

**1972**—The first asphalt was removed from the parking lot in front of the Yosemite Valley Visitor Center. The area was converted to use as a pedestrian mall.

**1974**—Hang gliding was officially allowed from Glacier Point, and 170 flights were made.

**1976**—The Tioga Road opened April 10, its earliest opening on record.

**1980**—The Yosemite General Management Plan was completed and approved. It was the first systematically developed, long-range planning document for the park.

**1981**—Captive-born peregrine falcon chicks were successfully reared in a nest on El Capitan.

**1983**—The first-ever prescribed burn was accomplished in the Mariposa Grove of Big Trees.

*Early ranger-naturalist program, probably in 1920s*

**1984**—Yosemite was named to the World Heritage List. The California Wilderness Bill designated 94% of the park as wilderness.

**1986**—California bighorn sheep were reintroduced into Yosemite.

**1987**—Park visitation exceeded three million for the first time; 3,266,342 visitors were recorded.

**1990**—Yosemite celebrated its 100th birthday as a national park. Major forest fires raked the park during August.

**1992**—Delaware North Company was awarded the Yosemite concession contract by the National Park Service.

**1995**—The Yosemite Wilderness Center opened its doors, and the wilderness permit reservation system was initiated.

**1996**—A massive rockfall occurred in Yosemite Valley between Washburn and Glacier Points. The slide downed several hundred trees, damaged the Happy Isles Nature Center, and killed one visitor.

**1997**—In early January, major flooding occurred in Yosemite Valley; some 450 campsites, 350 motel and cabin units, and 200 concessioner housing units were lost. The estimated cost of repairing the damage was $178 million. Yosemite Valley remained closed to visitors for three months.

**1999**—Camp Curry celebrated its 100th anniversary.

**2000**—The Yosemite Valley Plan, the management document to guide future development, was completed.

## Historical Sites in Yosemite Valley

The following locations have special historical significance or were the sites of early development in Yosemite Valley. They are listed in order of locale beginning at the west end of the valley, continuing to the east along Southside Drive, focusing on the east end of Yosemite Valley, then heading back to the west along Northside Drive. In your explorations, remember that all cultural resources should be left unimpaired, and that digging and use of metal detectors are not allowed. Marker references are to small wooden posts that have been placed along valley roads to indicate particular landmarks or attractions. See the map below for details.

### Bridalveil Meadow (Marker V-13).
This spot is where the Mariposa Battalion camped in March of 1851. The party was in search of Indians and was the first group of whites ever to enter Yosemite Valley. Around a campfire here, the group proposed and applied the name "Yo-sem-ite" to this marvel of Nature's handiwork. It was also here that President Teddy Roosevelt and John Muir camped in 1903 and discussed the need to preserve our nation's wilderness areas.

### Bridalveil Fall (Marker V-14 *that is just past the turnoff for Wawona).* This is roughly the place where the wagon road from Wawona entered Yosemite Valley. Towards the Merced River through the trees, a large sewer plant operated for many years. The sewer plant was removed in 1987, and over three acres were freed of development. Yosemite Valley sewage is now carried by pipeline to a new processing facility in El Portal.

### El Capitan View (watch for Marker V-17 *in a parking area on the left where trees grow out of the asphalt).* Just upriver from here is the site of the bear feeding platform used in the 1920s and '30s. Garbage was dumped on the lighted platform that drew feeding bears and gawking tourists each night. Enlightened managers have long since dispensed with the spectacle.

### Sentinel Rock View (Marker V-18 *about 1.4 miles past El Capitan View on the right and left).* Here was a portion of Lower Yosemite Village, which included the Yosemite Chapel (later moved to its present location east of here), Leidig's Hotel that operated from 1869 to 1888, and Camp Ahwahnee (1908-15). This is also the trailhead for James McCauley's Four-Mile Trail to Glacier Point, where for several years a tollhouse was maintained to collect fees from hikers and horseback riders. Watch for the locust trees that are the only remnants of this earlier occupation.

### Swinging Bridge Turnout *(there is no marker here, but the turnout is about a quarter-mile past V-18 on the left).* The remainder of Lower Yosemite Village was located here. Black's Hotel stood from 1869 through 1888, photographer George Fiske's residence and studio were near the river to the west, Galen Clark had a residence here, and the Coffman & Kenney Stables operated for several years. As well, a boardwalk nearly a half-mile in length was constructed through the meadow to the east to connect the Upper and Lower Village areas.

### Chapel Parking Area (Marker V-20 *about one-half mile beyond Swinging Bridge on the right).* This area was covered by extensive development from the 1860s until the 1950s. Here were the Upper Hotel (known at various times as Hutchings House, the Sentinel Hotel, and the Yosemite Falls Hotel), photographic studios (Boysen's, Foley's, and Pillsbury's), Best's Studio, Degnan's Store and Restaurant, the world-famous Cosmopolitan Saloon, the Village Store, and many other structures. In 1925, the "new" Yosemite Village site (the present location) was selected, and an administration building, museum, post office, and several artist studios were built. Slowly the Upper (old) Village was dismantled and razed. The Village Store was the last major building to go in 1959. The observant historian can still find plenty of evidence of Yosemite's yesteryears with a little exploring here.

## Stoneman Meadow (Marker V-23

*near Curry Village).* This meadow has been the center of much activity over the years. Within it stood a large wooden hotel called the Stoneman House built by the State of California in 1886 that burned in 1896. James Lamon, a homesteader in the park's earliest days, built a cabin near here, and planted two apple orchards in 1859. One now serves as the Curry Village parking lot, the other is behind the Curry Stables (shuttle bus stop #18). Stoneman Meadow will also be remembered as the site of a riot in 1970 which pitted young people against N.P.S. personnel in a clash over curfews, noise levels, and lifestyles.

## The Ahwahnee Hotel *(Shuttle bus stop #3).* Before the present hotel was built, an active stable business was operated at this spot. Known as Kenneyville, the stable was extensive and there were horses, shops, barns, and houses mingled here. When automobile travel became popular, the need for such a large stable was eliminated. In 1926, to make way for The Ahwahnee, the stable was moved to its present location and the old buildings torn down. Many people are unaware that during World War II between 1943 and 1945 the Ahwahnee Hotel was closed to the public and converted to use as a Naval Convalescent Hospital. During that time almost 7,000 patients were rehabilitated.

## Yosemite Cemetery *(Just west of and across the street from the Yosemite Museum in Yosemite Village).* This is the cemetery where, upon their deaths, local residents were buried between the 1870s and the 1950s. There's a wide variety of personalities interred here, from Native Americans like Indian Lucy and Sally Ann Castagnetto to pioneer settlers and innkeepers like Galen Clark and James Mason Hutchings. A guide to the cemetery is on sale at the Visitor Center.

## Yosemite Falls (Marker V-3). In the forested area between the parking lot and Lower Yosemite Fall, James Mason Hutchings built a sawmill for preparation of lumber to upgrade his hotel. John Muir was employed to run the sawmill for a time, and constructed a cabin nearby to house himself. It featured running water: one strand of Yosemite Creek flowed right through it. Camp Yosemite, also known as Camp Lost Arrow, stood near the base of the fall and to its east from 1901 until 1915.

## Yosemite Lodge (Marker V-4). The lodge area was first developed as Army headquarters for the park in 1906. The facility included two large barracks buildings, two bath houses and lavatories, 156 tent frames, and a parade ground. When the Army administration ended in 1914, so did the need for the headquarters, and they were converted to accommodate visitors in 1915.

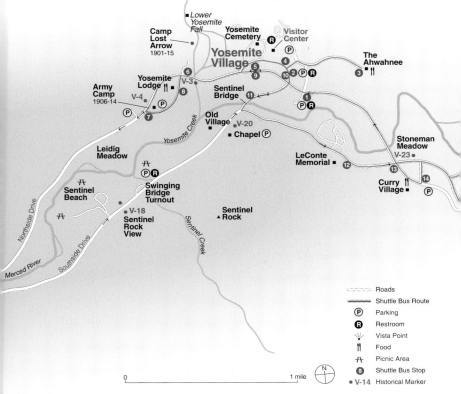

## Yosemite's Future

### A Plan for the 21st Century

For at least the past thirty years, National Park Service managers have worked to develop a plan to guide Yosemite's development in the coming century. In 1980, the "General Management Plan" was issued and approved. Since then, however, only a relatively few elements of that plan have been implemented.

In fall of 2000, a document that focused on Yosemite Valley was released to supplement the General Management Plan. The "Yosemite Valley Plan" incorporated a number of pending planning efforts including the Merced Wild and Scenic River Plan, the Concession Services Plan, the Yosemite Valley Housing Plan, the Yosemite Lodge Development Concept Plan, and the Yosemite Falls Project. The recovery program following the major flooding of 1997 also became tied up in the plan.

Needless to say, the planning process has been complicated and time-consuming. Further, several law suits have slowed the approval of various documents, which are still not okayed for final implementation. Once the Yosemite Valley Plan goes forward, there will be similar planning efforts for other parts of the park.

### Details of the Yosemite Valley Plan

The Yosemite Valley Plan would restore approximately 176 developed and disturbed acres in Yosemite Valley to natural conditions. In addition, 173 acres of developed land would be developed to accommodate visitor and employee services such as campgrounds, day-visitor parking, and employee housing. There would be more campsites and fewer lodging units than there are now.

The plan would consolidate parking for day visitors at Yosemite Village, where a new Valley Visitor Center would be located, and in parking areas outside Yosemite Valley. There would be a major reduction in vehicle travel in the eastern portion of Yosemite Valley during periods of peak visitation.

The area of former Upper River and Lower River Campgrounds would be restored to a mosaic of meadow, riparian, and California black oak woodland communities. Roads would be removed from Ahwahnee and Stoneman Meadows, and parking and fruit trees would be removed from Curry Orchard and the area restored to natural conditions.

Southside Drive would be converted to two-way traffic from El Capitan crossover to Curry Village, and Northside Drive would be closed to motor vehicles and converted to a multi-use (bicycle and pedestrian) paved trail from El Capitan crossover to Yosemite Lodge.

There would be minimal new development west of Yosemite Lodge. The net effect of the plan would be to reduce development in Yosemite Valley by 71 acres.

### Key Questions for Yosemite's Future

- As the population of the Central Valley of California continues to grow, how will park managers contend with 4 to 5 million people living within a two-hour drive of Yosemite?

- Should and will the National Park Service impose limits on access to the park to ensure the quality of each visitor's experience?

- Will a regional agency ever be put in place to monitor the effects on Yosemite of road construction, logging, suburbanization, global climate change, acid and nutrient rain, and other impacts that originate outside the park?

- Should and will the National Park Service eliminate motor vehicle use in Yosemite?

- Should an annual limit be placed on total number of visitors to Yosemite? Is the appropriate number 4 million, 6 million, 8 million, or more?

### Yosemite's Original Management Plan

When Yosemite Valley and the Mariposa Grove were set aside as a public reserve by the federal government in 1864, the State of California was charged with creating a commission to administer the new grant. Noted landscape architect Frederick Law Olmsted was delegated the job of preparing a report and setting out the policy that should guide the management of the grant.

Olmsted's management plan was a visionary document. Among his key points was that: "The first requirement is to preserve the natural scenery and restrict within the narrowest limits the necessary accommodation of visitors." In elaborating, he stated: "Structures should not detract from the dignity of the scene. In preventing the sacrifice of anything that should be of the slightest value to visitors to the convenience, bad taste, playfulness, carelessness, or wanton destructiveness of present visitors, would probably yield in each case the interest of uncounted millions to the selfishness of a few."

When Yosemite's management plan is finally completed and approved, it will be interesting to see whether Olmsted's recommendations have been heeded.

## The Yosemite Hall of Fame

### Chief Tenaya

When Euro-Americans first visited Yosemite Valley in 1851, they encountered the Yosemite Indians. Their leader was Chief Tenaya. He has been called not only a brave warrior but an unusual personality who maintained his authority over his people by his native influence and the respect that he commanded.

Accounts have it that a tribal shaman warned Tenaya that "horsemen of the lowlands" (probably a reference to the Spaniards) represented the gravest threat to his people and should be guarded against. When in 1849 gold miners began entering the foothills and interacting with the native residents, Tenaya apparently felt threatened. He reportedly informed the invading whites that the Yosemites would be peaceable, but only if they could continue to occupy Yosemite Valley and not be disturbed.

Such an arrangement was obviously unacceptable to the new foothill residents. The Mariposa Battalion was dispatched to subdue the Yosemites, but met with only limited success. In May of 1851, the greatest portion of the band was rounded up and marched to a reservation in the Central Valley. Problems arose, the federal government never ratified a treaty, and by the end of the year, Tenaya and his people had either escaped or been permitted to return to Yosemite Valley.

The following year, Indians in the valley allegedly attacked a party of miners, and further efforts to remove them resulted. Tenaya's group fled to the high country of Yosemite and to the east side again. In 1853, they returned once more to Yosemite Valley, but their fate was practically sealed.

Despite his best efforts, Tenaya, the last chief of the Yosemites, was unable to protect his people and their homeland from the incursions of the whites. He was killed by stoning late in 1853. There are two versions of his death, but the most commonly accepted is that the Yosemites stole horses from their eastern Sierran neighbors, who attacked in retribution. Tenaya's name is common in the park today having been attached to a canyon, a lake, and other features.

### Galen Clark

Known as the "Guardian of Yosemite," Galen Clark was as intimately involved in Yosemite's early history as any other person. He moved to the park in 1856 at the age of 42 suffering from a debilitating lung disease that doctors had indicated would quickly end his life. The Yosemite fresh air and inspiring scenery must have been therapeutic; Clark lived to be 95.

He first homesteaded at Wawona, developing his place as a stopping point on the stage route to Yosemite (Clark's Station). He visited the Mariposa Grove of Big Trees in 1857 with Milton Mann, then explored the trees and publicized them. He recognized the value and uniqueness of the sequoias and Yosemite Valley, and worked to bring about the enactment of the Yosemite Grant, the 1864 law that set aside the Yosemite Valley and Mariposa Big Trees as the world's first state park.

In 1866, Galen Clark became the first "Yosemite Guardian," employed by the State of California to oversee the grant. He continued in this job until the political winds changed in 1880 and a new Guardian was employed. He worked odd jobs for nine years and then was hired once again to be the Yosemite Guardian. His second term lasted seven years, and he closed out his life by guiding, writing books about the park, and helping wherever he could.

As Guardian, Clark made many needed improvements, worked to relocate homesteaders, and persevered in his efforts to protect Yosemite. John Muir called him "the best mountaineer I ever met . . . one of the most sincere tree-lovers I ever knew." Following his death, he was buried in the Yosemite Cemetery in a grave shaded by sequoias he planted himself and headed by a granite marker bearing his self-chiseled name.

## James Mason Hutchings

James Mason Hutchings will be remembered most for being Yosemite's first and best publicist. A native of England, he was attracted to Yosemite Valley very soon after its original entry by whites. In 1855, he organized and led the first "tourist" party to visit the valley, bringing with him the artist Thomas Ayres who sketched the first non-Indian illustrations of Yosemite's wonders. Hutchings published the sketches and paired them with his descriptions of the place, drawing national attention to a previously unknown scenic treasure.

When his health failed, he, too, chose to come to Yosemite, and in 1862 purchased an existing hotel that became known as Hutchings House. The hotel was very primitive; only sheets of muslin hung to separate the rooms. Hutchings built a sawmill along Yosemite Creek to prepare the lumber for more effective partitions, and for a time employed John Muir to run the mill.

When the Yosemite Grant was set aside in 1864, Hutchings became embroiled in lengthy and bitter litigation with the government as a property owner dispossessed. His political fortunes changed, however, in 1880 when he was named to succeed Galen Clark as Yosemite Guardian. He worked in that capacity for four years.

Hutchings' many writings will live after him. His *Hutchings California Magazine* is full of historical gems, and he published a series of handbooks entitled *Guide to the Yosemite Valley and the Big Trees*. His most famous work is *In the Heart of the Sierras*, which is representative of the best travel writing of that era.

Killed in a wagon accident on the Old Big Oak Flat Road in Yosemite Valley in 1902, Hutchings is buried in the Yosemite Cemetery.

## John Muir

For his efforts on behalf of the park, John Muir has come to be recognized as the most significant individual in the history of Yosemite. This reputation is certainly deserved; Muir's contributions to the place through the years were considerable, particularly his efforts to create

Yosemite National Park in 1890. He will also long be associated with the park thanks to his eloquent, loving writings.

John Muir first visited Yosemite in 1868 and returned the following summer to work as a shepherd in what would later become the park's high country. Late in 1869, he could no longer resist the lure of Yosemite Valley and found work doing odd jobs there for James Mason Hutchings. He built a small cabin on Yosemite Creek and began a long-term residence in his beloved Yosemite.

Muir roamed and studied the park, learning its aspects as intimately as he could. He became renowned as a guide, and entertained such visitors as Asa Gray, William Keith, Ralph Waldo Emerson, and other luminaries of the day. His marathon hikes with few or no provisions have become legendary. All along he recorded his experiences and documented the natural world around him in a series of journals.

In 1871, Muir published a newspaper article about Yosemite; it was the first of a series of articles and books he would write during his life. Topics of his writing included the glaciers, the forests, winter storms, and everything else about Yosemite that came to fascinate him. In the mid-'70s, he moved from Yosemite, married, and began a new life in Martinez.

In 1889, he returned to the park with Robert Underwood Johnson. It was during this visit that the two hatched a campaign to establish Yosemite National Park. Using articles, personal visits, and other lobbying efforts, the two saw the 1890 act to create the national park through to its successful passage.

Muir was later to write *My First Summer in the Sierra* and *The Yosemite* (among many others), both of which would become Yosemite classics. His tireless work in opposition to the damming of the park's Hetch Hetchy Valley (a fight that he lost), drained him physically and contributed to his death in 1914.

## David and Jennie Curry

The Curry name is synonymous with the concession operation in Yosemite, and these lively people were pioneer innkeepers in the park. In 1899, they moved to California from Indiana and established a small camp in the eastern end of Yosemite Valley. Starting with seven tents for guests and a dining tent that seated twenty, the Currys initiated an enterprise that experienced immediate growth.

By the end of their first season, the camp size had increased to 25 tents, and almost 300 guests had been accommodated. The operation soon became known as Camp Curry, and thanks to their warm hospitality and outgoing personalities, the Currys prospered.

David Curry specialized in entertaining his guests with both disarming informality and brash showmanship. Every night at the campfire, people were encouraged to add wood to the fire, and while it burned, to tell stories or lead songs. Curry also revitalized the "Fire Fall," the spectacle that involved pushing burning embers from the brink of Glacier Point to create a stream of fire down the cliff face.

"Mother" Curry, as she was affectionately called, was considerably less flamboyant, but continued the Camp Curry tradition when David died in 1917. She was assisted by various family members and saw her camp grow to include lodging for 1,300 guests.

In 1925, the Curry Camping Company and the Yosemite National Park Company merged to form a single concession operation known as the Yosemite Park & Curry Co. that operated until 1993.

## Ansel Adams

The man who best communicated the beauty of Yosemite through photography during the twentieth century was Ansel Adams, and his influence continues to be felt. His images have been a source of inspiration, delight, and enjoyment to millions of persons, and they have defined the Yosemite landscape for many. Further, he was a dogged conservationist who worked hard to protect the environment he photographed with such skill.

Interestingly, Ansel Adams was a gifted artist in two fields. He almost became a professional pianist, but the camera won out, particularly as Adams became more and more attached to Yosemite. He moved to the valley in 1920 to run the Sierra Club Lodge, and made the acquaintance of the proprietor of Best's Studio, painter Harry Best, who allowed Ansel the use of a piano. It brought Adams in contact with Best's daughter Virginia, whom he later married.

For several years, Adams worked as a "commercial" photographer doing publicity pictures for the Curry Co. and other such jobs. As the years passed, his promotional work gave way increasingly to his more "artistic" expression. His prints were offered for sale in gift shops and at Best's Studio, and before long he was gaining national recognition for his fine landscape work.

Many of his photographs were used to illustrate the beauty of natural areas that environmental groups hoped to have protected by Congress, and he undertook special assignments from the National Park Service to photograph the national parks. His landscapes became well-known for their detail, tonal ranges, unique composition, and fine printing. A multitude of awards were bestowed upon Adams for his photographic excellence.

He remained active as a photographer and conservationist until his death in 1984, teaching, lecturing, lobbying, and making new images all the while. Best's Studio is now operated as the Ansel Adams Gallery, and a peak on Yosemite's eastern boundary was named for him in 1985.

## Selected Yosemite Place Names

**Ahwahnee:** The native Indians' name for both a large village near Yosemite Falls and for the greater Yosemite Valley. Those Indians were known as the Ahwahnechees. Lafayette Bunnell reported that the name meant deep, grassy valley, although this is unsubstantiated. Some linguists believe that "place of a gaping mouth" is a closer translation.

**Big Oak Flat:** A small town near Yosemite's northwestern boundary from which the Highway 120 route took its original name. The massive oak (reportedly ten feet in diameter) that inspired the name is long since dead, the victim of miners' axes in the 1860s.

**Chilnualna:** This name, common in the Wawona area, is of unknown origin and meaning. An unsupported theory suggests its meaning is leaping water.

**Clark:** Yosemite Valley's first guardian in 1864 and the discoverer of the Mariposa Grove of Big Trees was Galen Clark. His name now graces a mountain, a mountain range, and other features in Yosemite.

**Conness:** A senator from California in the 1860s, John Conness introduced the bill in Congress that set aside Yosemite Valley and the Mariposa Grove of Big Trees as a state preserve. Mount Conness is an imposing peak on the park boundary north of Tioga Pass.

**Crane Flat:** Most probably named for a group of sand hill cranes encountered there by Lafayette Bunnell (John Muir also noted cranes at the location), although some assert the origin was a man named Crean who at one time resided at the spot.

**Curry:** David and Jennie "Mother" Curry established a small tent camp for the public in Yosemite Valley in 1899. It grew to become Camp Curry and later Curry Village. The merger of their operation with the Yosemite Park Company resulted in the Yosemite Park & Curry Co., a longtime concessioner.

**Dana:** J. D. Whitney's California Geological Survey named a prominent peak east of Tuolumne Meadows for James Dwight Dana in 1863. Dana was a Yale professor and considered the foremost American geologist of his time.

**El Capitan:** This massive granite cliff was named by the Mariposa Battalion in 1851. It is the Spanish equivalent of the native Indian name Too-tok-ah-noo-lah meaning Rock Chief or Captain. Other names assigned to the rock at one time or another were Crane Mountain and Giant's Tower (go Giants!).

**El Portal:** This is Spanish for gateway or entrance, and was used to name the terminus of the Yosemite Valley Railroad on the park's western doorstep. Now a small town on Highway 140, the site is slated to become the park's headquarters. Because of its searing summer heat, some have dubbed the place "Hell Portal."

**Glen Aulin:** James McCormick, at the behest of R. B. Marshall of the U.S.G.S., named this idyllic spot on the Tuolumne River with the Gaelic phrase for beautiful valley or glen in the early 1900s. A High Sierra Camp was built there in 1927.

**Half Dome:** Credit the Mariposa Battalion with describing this split mountain as a half dome. Of all the landmarks in Yosemite, Half Dome has worn the most names over the years, among them Rock of Ages, North Dome, South Dome, Sentinel Dome, Tis-sa-ack, Cleft Rock, Goddess of Liberty, Mt. Abraham Lincoln, and Spirit of the Valley. Somehow a t-shirt imprinted with the phrase "I climbed on top of the Goddess of Liberty" wouldn't quite work.

**Happy Isles:** One of Yosemite Valley's early Guardians named the three small islets on the Merced River for the emotions he enjoyed while exploring them ("no one can visit them without for the while forgetting the grinding strife of his world and being happy"). For years this was the site of a fish hatchery.

**Hetch Hetchy:** At one time a remarkably beautiful companion valley to Yosemite, Hetch Hetchy bears an Indian name that has been interpreted to have several meanings. The most popular is a kind of grass or plant with edible seeds that abounded in the valley, although some believe Hetchy means tree and Hetch Hetchy is descriptive of two yellow pine trees that grew at the entrance to the place. Hetch Hetchy was dammed by the damned City of San Francisco in the 1920s.

**Illilouette:** This French sounding name is actually an English translation (poor indeed!) of the Indian word Too-lool-a-we-ack. James Mason Hutchings opined that its meaning is "the place beyond which was the great rendezvous of the Yosemite Indians for hunting deer" (the great Miwok hunt club in the sky?).

**Lembert:** John Baptiste Lembert was an early settler in the Tuolumne Meadows region. He built a cabin at the soda springs in Tuolumne, and his name is attached to the granite dome nearby.

**Lyell:** Yosemite's highest peak (13,114 feet) was named for Sir Charles Lyell, an eminent English geologist, by the California Geological Survey in 1863.

**Mariposa:** The Spanish word for butterfly first applied to a land grant, later to the community, and then to the county. Because they occurred in Mariposa County when Galen Clark discovered them in 1857, the sequoias at the south end of Yosemite were called the Mariposa Grove of Big Trees.

**Merced:** The Spanish name given the river originating in Yosemite's high country when it was crossed in the San Joaquin Valley by the Moraga party. Formally known as El Rio de Nuestra Señora de la Merced (River of Our Lady of Mercy), the title was applied five days after the feast day of Our Lady of Mercy in 1806. All other names utilizing Merced in Yosemite are derived from the river's name.

**Mono:** Derived from the Yokuts Indian word monoi or monai meaning flies. At what is now known as Mono Lake, the resident Indians harvested, ate, and traded millions of the pupae of a fly—a favorite foodstuff of the native people of the region. The Shoshonean tribe grew to be known as the Mona or Mono Indians, and many landmarks east of Yosemite bear this name.

**Nevada:** Assigned as a name to the waterfall on the Merced River by the Mariposa Battalion in 1851. The word signifies snow in Spanish, and members of the battalion felt that the name was appropriate because the fall was so close to the Sierra Nevada and because the white, foaming water was reminiscent of a vast avalanche of snow.

**Olmsted:** A turnout with a remarkable view from the Tioga Road near Tenaya Lake was named for both Frederick Law Olmsted and his son, Frederick Law Olmsted, Jr. The senior Olmsted was involved in the earliest development of the 1864 Yosemite Grant, and served as Chairman of the first Board of Yosemite Valley Commissioners. His son worked as an N.P.S. planner in Yosemite and had a position on the Yosemite Advisory Board.

**Sierra Nevada:** This is the Spanish phrase for snowy mountain range. It was applied to California's greatest range of mountains by Father Pedro Font who glimpsed it from near Antioch in 1776. Because the word Sierra implies a series of mountains, it is both grammatically and politically incorrect to use the term "Sierras." If you do you will be castigated by self-righteous Yosemite word snobs.

**Stoneman:** A large hotel built by the State of California in 1885 once stood in the meadow just north of Curry Village. Known as the Stoneman House for then-Governor George Stoneman, it burned in 1896. The meadow and nearby bridge still bear the name.

**Tenaya:** The chief of the resident Indian tribe when the Mariposa Battalion entered Yosemite Valley in 1851 was named Tenieya. The battalion first encountered the Native Americans living near the banks of a lake near Tuolumne Meadows that they called Tenaya Lake.

**Tioga:** This in an Iroquois Indian word meaning where it forks, swift current, or gate. Miners at work on the Sierra crest near Yosemite established the Tioga Mining District in 1878, apparently importing the name from Pennsylvania or New York.

**Tuolumne:** An Indian tribe residing in the Sierra foothills near Knights Ferry was known as "Taulamne," reportedly pronounced Tu-ah-lum'-ne. The Indian name was applied to the river originating in Yosemite that flowed through their territory.

**Vogelsang:** Col. Benson, an Army officer and acting Superintendent of Yosemite National Park from 1905 to 1908, named a peak south of Tuolumne Meadows for either Alexander Vogelsang or his brother Charles Vogelsang, both of whom were affiliated with California Fish and Game. Vogelsang is German for meadow in which birds sing, an apt description of the site of the Vogelsang High Sierra Camp.

**Wawona:** The popular opinion is that the word is the Indian name for "big tree." The Indians viewed the trees as sacred and called them Woh-woh'-nah. The word is formed in imitation of the hooting of an owl, which bird to the native people was the guardian spirit and deity of the sequoias.

**White Wolf:** A meadow on the old route of the Tioga Road was named by John Meyer, who, while chasing Indians, came to the temporary camp of the band's chief. His name was White Wolf.

**Yosemite:** This name was assigned to the world's most beautiful valley by the Mariposa Battalion in 1851. They believed that the Yosemite people (as they were apparently known) who resided there should have their tribe's name perpetuated in the designation of the valley. The exact meaning of the name is disputed, but Lafayette Bunnell, a member of the battalion, later wrote that the term signified "grizzly bear." He was informed that because grizzly bears frequented the territory occupied by the Yosemites and because the Indian band was skilled at killing the bears, the name was taken as an appropriate one for the tribe.

### Further Reading

*Yosemite Place Names* by Peter Browning. Lafayette, CA: Great West Books, 1988.

*Place Names of the High Sierra* by Francis Farquhar. San Francisco: Sierra Club, 1926 (out of print).

## Getting to Yosemite

*M*ost visitors to Yosemite arrive in private automobiles, but there are public transportation alternatives. Below are brief descriptions of those various alternatives. They are followed by detailed descriptions of the highway routes to Yosemite. If you need further information about transportation to Yosemite National Park, call (209) 372-0200.

**By Air:** The largest air terminal close to Yosemite served by a number of major airlines and several smaller ones is Fresno's. Formerly known as FAT (Fresno Air Terminal), the facility has been upgraded to the Fresno Yosemite International Airport (FYI). At this time there is no bus connection to the park, and a rental car (from several major car rental agencies in the terminal) is required for the two-hour trip to Yosemite Valley. A small airline also flies to Merced. Bus service is available from the Merced Airport on VIA/Gray Line daily. Call (209) 384-1315, or in California, 1-800-369-7275 (the web address is www.via-adventures.com). Rental cars also are available in Merced.

**By Train:** Train transportation is available to Yosemite from both Northern and Southern California. The Northern California AMTRAK train, originating in Emeryville, carries passengers to Merced daily. Connection to Yosemite is made via the VIA/Gray Line bus. For the return to Emeryville, an AMTRAK train departs Merced every afternoon.

There are Southern California trains from both Los Angeles and San Diego on AMTRAK. The trip requires bus inter-connects from Los Angeles to Bakersfield and from Merced to Yosemite. Return travelers can catch a VIA/Gray Line bus to Merced for the AMTRAK trip to Bakersfield and connections to Las Vegas and Southern California. For train and bus reservations call 1-800-USA-RAIL.

**By Bus:** For those staying in visitor accommodations surrounding the park, there is a car-free option. The Yosemite Area Regional Transportation System (YARTS) provides bus service from many of the communities outside Yosemite. Along the Highway 140 route, service is available from Merced, Catheys Valley, Mariposa, Midpines, and El Portal. From Highways 120 and 132, buses can be caught in Coulterville, Greeley Hill, Groveland, and Buck Meadows. Service also is available from Mammoth Lakes over Highway 120 during summer months only. For information, call toll free to (877) 989-2787, or visit www.yosemite.com/yarts.

As noted above, VIA/Gray Line offers routes from Merced on a daily basis.

Reservations should be made by calling (209) 384-1315, or in California, 1-800-369-7275 (the web address is www.via-adventures.com).

**By Automobile:** There are four major routes to Yosemite National Park. What follows are points of interest, restaurants, and motels along each route. The list is not meant to be complete or exhaustive; rather, it reflects the preferences of the author. Because motels and restaurants are often short-lived, be sure to call ahead to avoid disappointment. Note: All directions and orientations assume that one is traveling toward Yosemite.

### HIGHWAY 41 FROM FRESNO

**Oakhurst** (45 miles north of Fresno):

*Points of Interest*

**Yosemite Sierra Visitor Center:** : On the right side of Highway 41 on the way out of town (just past El Cid restaurant). A great place to get oriented, ask for directions, and find books and maps about Yosemite.

**Fresno Flats Historical Park:** Turn right at the second Oakhurst stop light. Continue about half a mile to School Road (Road 427). Turn left and follow signs to this museum that includes a collection of old buildings depicting the lives of early settlers in the area. Hours are 1-3 p.m., Wednesday through Sunday.

*Restaurants*

**Crab Cakes:** 40278 Stagecoach Road (on the left, just past the second stop light, behind Subway), (559) 641-7667. Besides the namesake crab cakes, this small, well-run eatery serves fresh fish and shell fish, steak, chicken, and pasta. Meals include a bowl of delicious cole slaw and plenty of fresh bread. Patio seating is available.

**Old Mexico Taqueria:** Raley's Shopping Center (at the intersection of Highways 41 and 49), (559) 683-2777. This inexpensive outlet offers a lengthy menu of Mexican fare, and they prepare your choice as you wait in line. There are vegetarian options, and beer and wine are available.

**Szechuan Restaurant:** 40484 Highway 41 (on left, just south of the Best Western Motel), (559) 683-8328. Very acceptable Chinese food that's right off the highway and right on the price. "Spicy" alternatives are available throughout the menu, and they claim to use no MSG.

**Erna's Elderberry House & Bistro:** Highway 41 & Victoria Lane (on left on final descent into Oakhurst), (559) 683-6800. This is the proverbial diamond in the proverbial diamond in the foothill rough. One of the few 5-star rated restaurants in California, featuring old European cuisine with a California twist. Craig Claiborne of the *New York Times* spent three days here and wrote rave reviews. But beware, you must dress up and dinners run about $72 per person.

**Oka Japanese Restaurant:** 40291 Junction Drive (turn left onto Highway 49, turn right at first stop light), (559) 642-4850. Despite the walls painted with fish and other slightly odd bits of décor, this is a good place for sushi, and features first-rate, generally authentic food.

### Motels

**Oakhurst Lodge:** 40302 Highway 41 (on the left just past Oakhurst's second stop light), 1-800-OK-LODGE. 60 units; rates for two are $45-50 in winter, $60-65 spring and fall, and $70-80 in summer. The web address is www.oklodge.com.

**Shilo Inn:** 40644 Highway 41 (on the left past Oakhurst's second stop light), (559) 683-3555. 80 mini-suite units, pool; rates for two are $49-$69 in winter (except holidays), $79-$129 in summer. The web address is www.shiloinns.com/California/oakhurst.html.

**Yosemite Gateway Best Western:** 40530 Highway 41 (on the left past Oakhurst's second stop light), (559) 683-2378. 122 units, indoor and outdoor pools and spas, restaurant; rates for two are $45-$80 in winter; $80-$100 in summer. The web address is http://www.bestwestern.com.

**Holiday Inn Express:** 40662 Highway 41 (on the left past Oakhurst's second stop light), (559) 642-2525. 42 units, pool; rates for two are $39-$69 in winter; $79-$125 in summer.

**Chateau du Sureau:** Highway 41 & Victoria Lane (on left on final descent into Oakhurst), (559) 683-6860. Affiliated with Erna's Elderberry House (see restaurants above), this is very expensive, luxury lodging. 10 rooms, pool; rates for two are $350-$550. The web address is www.chateaudusureau.com.

| Mileages to Yosemite Valley |  |
| --- | --- |
| *Via Highway 41* | |
| From Los Angeles | 313 miles |
| From Bakersfield | 201 miles |
| From Fresno | 94 miles |
| From Oakhurst | 50 miles |
| From Fish Camp | 37 miles |
| *Via Highway 140* | |
| From Merced | 81 miles |
| From Mariposa | 43 miles |
| From El Portal | 14 miles |

Yosemite Falls

**Fish Camp** (15 miles north of Oakhurst):

### Points of Interest

**Yosemite Mountain-Sugar Pine Railroad:** 56001 Highway 41 (one mile south of Fish Camp on the right), (559) 683-7273. Take time out for a ride on a historic logging train. Utilizing Shay steam locomotives and Model A powered railcars, the railroad covers a four-mile loop. Many special events (including dinner trips) are offered throughout the year. A fee is charged for the ride.

### Restaurants

**The Narrow Gauge Inn:** 48571 Highway 41 (on the right just past the Yosemite Mt.-Sugar Pine Railroad, one mile south of Fish Camp), (559) 683-6446. A rustic but charming dining room with an excellent menu. Open April to October only.

**The Sierra Restaurant (at Tenaya Lodge):** 41122 Highway 41 (on the right as you enter Fish Camp), (559) 683-6555. Despite the p.r. department's claim that their "Sierra Alpine cuisine" borrows "heavily from the Native American and pioneering influences of the region," the food and service are actually pretty good.

### Motels

**Tenaya Lodge:** 41122 Highway 41 (on the right as you enter Fish Camp), (559) 683-6555. 244 rooms, indoor and outdoor pools, fitness center, cocktail lounge, restaurants; rates for two are $153-$165 in winter, $175-$190 in summer.

**Narrow Gauge Inn:** 48571 Highway 41 (on the right just past the Yosemite Mt.-Sugar Pine Railroad, one mile south of Fish Camp), (559) 683-7720. 27 rooms, pool; rates for two are $75-$105. The motel is open April through October.

## HIGHWAY 140 FROM MERCED

**Mariposa** (37 miles east of Merced):

### Points of Interest

**California State Mining & Mineral Museum:** 5007 Fairgrounds Road (on the left side of Highway 49 at the Mariposa County Fairgrounds, about 1 mile south of town), (209) 742-7625. A well-exhibited collection of minerals plus a mine tunnel and gold displays. An entrance fee is charged.

**Mariposa County Courthouse:** Bullion Street (turn right on 8th Street near the middle of town, then left on Bullion), (209) 966-4056. This handsome wooden building (erected in 1854) is the oldest courthouse in continuous use west of the Mississippi. Self-guided tours Monday through Friday.

**Mariposa History Center:** 5116 Jesse Street (on the left side of Highway 140 towards the east end of town and next to the Bank of America), (209) 966-2924. Historic displays and reconstructions of early-day Mariposa environments. Call for hours of operation.

### Restaurants

**Castillo's:** 4995 Fifth Street (one block off Highway 140; turn right at The Vault), (209) 742-4413. Castillo's is a good choice for regulation Mexican food. Outdoor seating available when weather permits.

**Savoury's:** 5027 Highway 140 (on the left side in the historic block downtown), (209) 966-7677. This small eatery has quickly become a favorite of the locals. A little cramped, but excellent food at moderate prices. Patio seating in summer.

**Charles Street Dinner House:** On the left of Highway 140 at Seventh Street downtown, (209) 966-2366. Good traditional food and plenty of it. A pretty sure bet.

### Motels

**Super 8 Motel:** 5059 Highway 140 (on left about midway through town), (209) 966-4288. 46 rooms; rates for two are $45-$65 in winter; $65-$170 in summer.

**Best Western Yosemite Way Station:** 4999 Highway 140 (on left where the highway intersects with Highway 49 South); (209) 966-7545. 78 rooms, pool; rates for two are $59-$85.

**Mariposa Lodge:** 5052 Highway 140 (on right about midway through town), (209) 966-3607. 44 rooms, pool, pets are allowed; rates for two are $55-$65 in winter; $65-$85 in summer.

**Mother Lode Lodge:** 5051 Highway 140 (on left about midway through town), (209) 966-2521. 14 rooms, pool, one kitchenette; rates for two are $48-$112. The web address is www.mariposamotel.com.

**Midpines** (10 miles east of Mariposa)

### Motels

**Yosemite Bug Hostel:** 6979 Highway 140 (on the left about two miles beyond "downtown" Midpines), (209) 966-6666. This alternative group of accommodations includes dorm cabins, family and private rooms with both shared and private baths, tent cabins, and campsites. The hostel is very popular with "backpacking" travelers and enjoys an international clientele. Rates vary by the season, and range from $16 plus tax for a dormitory bed to $115 plus tax for a private room. The Recovery Café offers inexpensive breakfasts and dinners, will pack a "trail lunch," and serves beer and wine. This establishment is affiliated with the American Youth Hostel program. The web address is www.yosemitebug.com.

*El Capitan in winter*

## El Portal (29 miles east of Mariposa):

### *Points of Interest*

**Site of Savage's Trading Post:** On the right side of Highway 140, 22 miles east of Mariposa, at the confluence of the South and Main Forks of the Merced River. This is the actual site of an early day trading post where the Indians and miners went for supplies and goods. There's a gift shop here now specializing in Indian arts and crafts. You'll also find the trailhead for a hike up the South Fork of the Merced that's ablaze with the colors of wildflowers in the spring. (209) 379-2301.

**Yosemite Rail Exhibit:** Turn left from Highway 140 onto El Portal Road and proceed one block to exhibit. Here are relics of early railroad activity in and around Yosemite, primarily old train cars and a locomotive. El Portal was the terminus of the Yosemite Valley Railroad.

### *Motels*

**Cedar Lodge:** On the right side of Highway 140, 25 miles east of Mariposa, (209) 379-2612. 122 rooms, pool, restaurant, bar; rates for two are $85-$129.

**Yosemite Redbud Lodge:** At the site of Savage's Trading Post, on the right side of Highway 140, 22 miles east of Mariposa, (800) 321-5261. This establishment was being completely remodeled at the time this book was going to press. Its operators plan to offer multi-day rentals in the renovated units.

**Yosemite View Lodge:** On the right side of Highway 140 at the park boundary line, (209) 379-2681. 278 rooms, gift shop, pools, restaurant; rates for two are $99-$139.

## HIGHWAY 120 FROM MANTECA

### Oakdale (20 miles east of Manteca):

### *Points of Interest*

**Hershey Chocolate Company:** 1400 S. Yosemite Avenue, (209) 847-0381. Free half-hour tours of the chocolate factory are conducted Monday through Friday from 8 a.m. until 3 p.m. See kisses wrapped and huge vats of chocolate, and you may even get a treat when you're done.

### Jamestown (32 miles east of Oakdale on Highway 108, about 6 miles east off the main route):

### *Points of Interest*

**Railtown 1897:** Fifth Avenue (just beyond town), (209) 984-4641. This is a State Historic Park featuring a 26-acre round-house and shop complex with steam locomotives and rolling passenger cars that have served the Sierra Railroad and Mother Lode since 1897. Open from 10 a.m. to 5 p.m. during summer and on weekends in winter.

**Downtown Jamestown:** Main Street Jamestown is lined with shops, restaurants, and galleries housed in restored historic buildings. The Gold Rush theme predominates in this thriving tourist attraction.

### *Restaurants*

**Jamestown Hotel:** On Main Street, downtown, (209) 984-3902. Serving "continental California cuisine" from 5 to 9 daily, with a Sunday brunch. Outdoor cafe in summer.

**Hotel Willow Restaurant:** Main and Willow, downtown, (209) 984-3998. Food for the "California gourmet" at dinner nightly. Good for families.

**Michelangelo:** On Main Street, downtown, (209) 984-4830. An interesting new Italian option in a quaint location. Full bar available.

*Bridalveil Fall*

### Moccasin (37 miles east of Oakdale on Highway 120):

### *Points of Interest*

**Moccasin Creek Fish Hatchery:** On the left side of Highway 49 about 100 feet south of its intersection with Highway 120, (209) 989-2312. Take a self-guided tour of this facility (operated by the California Department of Fish and Game), where 1,000,000 catchable size rainbow trout are produced annually for Sierra foothill reservoirs, streams, and rivers. Open 7:30 a.m. to 3 p.m. daily, year round.

### Groveland (9 miles east of Moccasin):

### *Restaurants*

**Hotel Charlotte:** On the left side of Highway 120 in the center of downtown, (209) 962-6455. They characterize their food as hearty California country cuisine. Open for dinner from April through October only. The web address is www.hotelcharlotte.com.

**Groveland Hotel Restaurant:** 18767 Main Street - on the right side of Highway 120, (209) 962-4000. Serving a varied menu prepared from California seasonal ingredients with herbs from the hotel's garden, and featuring an award-winning wine list. The web address is www.groveland.com/rest.htm.

*Motels*

**Groveland Hotel:** 18767 Main Street - on the right side of Highway 120, (209) 962-4000. 17 rooms and suites; rates for two are $135-$210 (including breakfast). Mid-week and winter specials are available. The web address is www.groveland.com.

**Buck Meadows** (12 miles east of Groveland):

*Restaurants*

**Buck Meadows Restaurant:** 7647 Highway 120 (on the left where the road gets wide), (209) 962-5281. Offering classic American cuisine, a variety of beer and wines, and daily specials.

*Motels*

**Best Value Yosemite Westgate Lodge:** 7633 Highway 120, (209) 962-5281. 55 rooms; rates for two are $59-$139, depending on season.

*Tioga Road view*

## HIGHWAY 120 FROM LEE VINING

**Lee Vining** (at intersection of Highways 120 and 395). A good web site for the area is www.monolake.org/chamber/.

*Points of Interest*

**Mono Lake County Park:** 5 miles north of Lee Vining on Highway 395. A great spot for a picnic with a trail down to the lakeshore.

**Mono Lake Information Center:** Downtown Lee Vining, (760) 647-6386. Operated by the Mono Lake Committee, the group primarily responsible for saving and restoring Mono Lake, this outlet offers free educational exhibits, slide shows, and movies to visitors, plus a good bookstore.

**Mono Lake Visitor Center:** Just north of town on the right side of Highway 395. This impressive multi-agency facility is replete with modern displays, exhibits, a bookstore, slide shows, and a great deck overlooking the lake. For the story of Mono Lake, this is a must visit. An admission fee is charged.

*Restaurants*

**Mono Inn**

**The Mono Inn Restaurant:** On Highway 395 five miles north of its junction with Highway 120, (760) 647-6581. This classic old inn overlooking the lake has been rehabilitated by the Ansel Adams family, and the food, décor, ambience, and view are terrific. Terrace dining is available in the summer. Open from April or May through October only. The web address is www.anseladams.com.

**Mono Mike's Barbecue:** Downtown Lee Vining, (760) 647-6432. Featuring ribs, chicken, burgers, and a front patio.

**Tioga Pass Resort:** Nine miles west of Lee Vining on Highway 120, (209) 372-4471. A local landmark, famous for its homemade pies (see page 70).

**Whoa Nellie Deli:** At intersection of Highways 120 and 395, (760) 647-1088. This somewhat strange establishment inside the Mobil Gas Mart features excellent food, including fish tacos, buffalo meatloaf, and lobster taquitos. You can even order a pitcher of margaritas.

*Motels*

**Best Western Lakeview Lodge:** On Highway 395 in downtown Lee Vining, (760) 647-6543 or (800) 528-1234. A nice motel run by even nicer people, the Banta's. 47 rooms, rates for 2 are $42-$112.

**Murphey's Motel:** On Highway 395 in downtown Lee Vining, (760) 647-6316. A decent motel with a AAA rating; one of the buildings is rustic, the other contemporary. 43 rooms, rates for two are $53-$108. The web address is www.murpheysyosemite.com.

**Tioga Pass Resort:** Nine miles west of Lee Vining on Highway 120, 372-4471. 10 housekeeping cabins and 4 motel-type units; rates for 2 are $100-175 per night, and $875-1075 per week.

| Mileages to Yosemite Valley | |
|---|---|
| *Via Highway 120 from the West* | |
| From San Francisco | 195 miles |
| From Sacramento | 176 miles |
| From Stockton | 127 miles |
| From Manteca | 117 miles |
| From Oakdale | 96 miles |
| From Groveland | 49 miles |
| *Via Highway 120 from the East* | |
| From Reno | 218 miles |
| From Carson City | 188 miles |
| From Bishop | 146 miles |
| From Mammoth Lakes | 106 miles |
| From Lee Vining | 74miles |

## Yosemite in Fiction

Since people started writing about it in the 1850s, Yosemite has figured as a grand locale for several works of fiction. From mass-appeal romances to beatnik epics to entangled mysteries, the array is an impressive one. The following is a list of some of the better and more unusual literary works with a Yosemite setting.

**1. The Forge of God** by Greg Bear. New York: Tom Doherty Associates, 1987. This science fiction novel is set in "futuristic" 1997 when there are profound changes to the solar system and the earth is threatened with destruction. People migrate to Yosemite to await their imminent demise. The book climaxes with an enormous cataclysm brought on by seismic disruptions. There's a great description of the collapse of the Royal Arches, the blockage of Yosemite Falls, the burial of Curry Village, and the destruction of Half Dome.

**2. Star Trek V: The Final Frontier** by J. M. Dillard. Based on the screenplay by David Loughery. New York: Pocket Books, 1989. Media spin-off in reverse. A book that grew out of the movie, part of which was filmed in the park. In one episode, McCoy, Spock, and Kirk are on "shore leave" in Yosemite. Captain Kirk attempts a free climb of El Capitan, apparently falls to his death, only to have Spock (wearing levitation boots) catch him by the ankles in mid-air.

**3. The Dharma Bums** by Jack Kerouac. New York: The Viking Press, 1958. The beat generation goes hiking! Here's a classic account of a 1955 climb of Yosemite's Matterhorn Peak by Kerouac, Gary Snyder, and John Montgomery, written as fiction. The description of two crazed beatniks bounding down the side of the Matterhorn, yodeling and laughing, is particularly joyful.

**4. The Affair of the Jade Monkey** by Clifford Knight. New York: Dodd, Mead & Co., 1943. A reprint edition was published by the Yosemite Association in 1993. Detective Huntoon Rogers tracks a suspicious character to Yosemite National Park. A body is found in the backcountry, so Rogers joins a 7-day hiking party. One of the hikers is murdered and a small jade monkey appears in another's pack. Can Huntoon solve the case and thwart an enemy plot directed against the nation?

**5. Angels of Light** by Jeffrey B. Long. New York: William Morrow & Co., 1987. Here's a Yosemite climbing novel with a twist. Its based loosely on the true story of the drug plane that crashed at Lower Merced Pass Lake in the park's backcountry. Before the rangers caught on, hundreds of pounds of marijuana were packed out by Yosemite climbers. The author characterizes it as the end of innocence for the park's climbing subculture.

**6. Images on Silver** by Rayanne Moore. Toronto: Harlequin Books, 1984. Believe it or not, a Harlequin Romance set in Yosemite. Christy Reilly is a highly-acclaimed wildlife photographer who meets Ranger Travis Jeffords. Travis keeps asking Christy why she has worked alone for so long. Christy's secret is something no man can understand.

**7. Fires of Innocence** by Jane Bonander. New York: St. Martin's Press, 1994. In a snowbound cabin in 1860s Yosemite Valley, Alex Golovin, a government attorney bent on buying up land for the national park, and Scotty MacDowell, daughter of a valley homesteader, come to know each other. Thrilling her with "searing kisses and teasing caresses," he will not let the "sensuous spitfire" stand in the way of his work. Steamy and far-fetched.

**8. Nurse in Yosemite** by Beatrice Warren. New York: Avalon Books, 1982. Nurse Doralee Dahlquist moves to Yosemite and takes a job at the medical clinic. All goes well until she falls for photographer Angus McGonigal. The conflict arises from fellow nurse Jan Stagnetto's claim that she will marry handsome Angus. Will Angus resist Jan's charms or will Doralee get dumped?

**9. A Body to Dye For** by Grant Michaels. New York: St. Martin's Press, 1990. Incredibly, this one's about a gay hairdresser/detective who finds the dead body of a Yosemite park ranger in the bed of one of his regular customers. In his efforts to solve the case, he follows leads back to Yosemite National Park, where his contacts in the gay world help him sort out a cast of colorful characters.

**10. High Sierra** by Nevada Barr. New York: Putnam & Sons, 2004. The famed national park mystery writer finally inserts her protagonist, Anna Pigeon, into Yosemite. She's working undercover as a waitress at The Ahwahnee, where her co-workers' odd behavior leads her into the backcountry and a showdown with some evil druggies. It's Yosemite as the "dark side."

*Pacific tree frog*

## Yosemite on the Internet

T hanks to the amazing growth of the Internet, there are now lots of online resources available for Yosemite. Whether found on sites that are maintained by the government or on the personal pages of passionate Yosemite lovers, Yosemite information, photographs, maps, and stories are abundant. Here are some of the best available at this time.

**Yosemite Online** - The Web Site of the Yosemite Association (www.yosemite.org). This full-featured site is best known for its web cam view of Yosemite Valley from Turtleback Dome, its extensive news archives, a variety of diary accounts about Yosemite, and an area dedicated to natural history issues in the Sierra. There's also an extensive Yosemite Store and visitor information.

**Yosemite National Park Home Page** (www.nps.gov/yose). This is the official park web site maintained by the National Park Service. It has lots of visitor information, nuts and bolts data, official government press releases, a section about park planning and management issues, programs for students, and a park map.

**DNC Parks & Resorts at Yosemite** (www.yosemitepark.com). Operated by the park's chief concessioner, this site is most important for the information it provides about lodging options in Yosemite. Recently, the capability to make room reservations online has been added, and a certain number of lodging units can only be reserved this way. There's also information about special events, discount offers, and jobs in the park.

**National Park Reservation System** (reservations.nps.gov). This site provides an easy and convenient way to make camping reservations (using a credit card) for Yosemite and other national park campgrounds. It certainly beats trying to use their phone-in system. Options are available for individual, family, and group sites at all campgrounds that require reservations (see page 12).

**Yosemite Trip Planning Online** (www.nps.gov/yose/trip/index.htm). These pages are part of the official National Park Service site for Yosemite. They encompass a range of topics designed to help visitors make plans for their trip to the park. One particularly helpful feature is the Current Conditions page, with links to the *Yosemite Today* newspaper and info on what's open, weather data, etc.

**Yosemite Wilderness Information** (www.nps.gov/yose/wilderness). This National Park Service site provides extensive information for backpackers, including trip planning ideas, bear avoidance techniques, trail data, hiking conditions, and most important, an online wilderness permit reservation option. While the site sometimes goes long periods without updating, there's good solid material available here.

**The Yosemite Fund** (www.yosemitefund.org). This is the major fundraising organization for Yosemite, and its site reports on the status of projects being undertaken, discusses volunteer opportunities, describes the hugely successful Yosemite license plate program, and allows persons to make donations on-line.

**The Yosemite Institute** (www.yni.org/yi/). This organization offers environmental education in the park, and their site offers a program orientation slide show, information about the educational curriculum, organizational data, and teacher resources. For school groups interested in a high-quality learning experience in Yosemite, this is the place to check.

**The Yosemite Store Online** (www.yosemitestore.com). For visitors interested in information, books, maps, gifts, and other Yosemite-related products, this site is made to order. The collection of items available is extensive, all products are illustrated in color, and the ordering process (with a credit card) is efficiently handled through a secure server. Yosemite Association members can take advantage of a 15% discount on anything they order, too.

**Yosemite Today Online** (www.nps.gov/yose/now/today.htm). This site allows prospective visitors to download as Adobe Reader files (PDF format) the park visitor handout known as *Yosemite Today*. It contains a calendar of guided programs and park activities, as well as hours of operation for visitor centers and museums.

*Tioga high country*